EVIDENCE OF PRACTICE

PLAYBOOK FOR VIDEO-POWERED PROFESSIONAL LEARNING

ADAM GELLER

WITH ANNIE LEWIS O'DONNELL

AFTERWORD BY JIM KNIGHT

Evidence of Practice

van Es, E. A., et al., Journal of Teacher Education Vol. 65(4)
p. 347 © 2014 by American Association of Colleges for Teacher Education
Reprinted by Permission of SAGE Publications, Inc.

For information about this title or to order other books and/or electronic media, contact the publisher:
R3 Collaboratives, 95 Third Street Floor 2, San Francisco CA 94103

http://www.evidenceofpractice.com

ISBN 978-0-9993781-0-6 (paperback)
ISBN 978-0-9993781-1-3 (e-book)
LCCN 2017955801

Publisher's Cataloging-In-Publication Data

Names: Geller, Adam. | O'Donnell, Annie Lewis, 1979- | Knight, Jim, writer of supplementary textual content.
Title: Evidence of practice : playbook for video-powered professional learning / Adam Geller, with Annie Lewis O'Donnell ; afterword by Jim Knight.
Description: San Francisco CA : R3 Collaboratives, [2017] | "O" in title word "of" is represented by a play button symbol. | Includes bibliographical references.
Identifiers: ISBN 9780999378106 (paperback) | ISBN 9780999378113 (ebook)
Subjects: LCSH: Teachers--In-service training. | Audio-visual education. | Professional education.
Classification: LCC LB1731 .G45 2017 (print) | LCC LB1731 (ebook) | DDC 370.71/1--dc23

Cover design: The Book Designers
Cover art: Morgunova Tetiana/Shutterstock
Interior design: 1106 Design

Printed in the United States of America

10   9   8   7   6   5   4   3   2   1

For Judy and Charles Geller, my first coaches

TABLE OF CONTENTS

PREFACE

I n my first-year year teaching in St. Louis, Missouri, I wanted nothing more than to be a *great* science teacher for my students. Unfortunately, no one in my building had science expertise. No one could give me real feedback or support. I was treading water trying to figure out how to teach science on my own.

Thankfully, I had the good fortune to meet Robert Powell from the Taylor Community Science Resource Center—an organization that partners with local schools to build high-quality science education opportunities for students. This was my professional development lifeline.

My school didn't have a contract for during-day support, so Robert agreed to meet with me after school at his office. Instead of fumbling through the concepts I needed to teach alone, we collaborated on plans for hands-on learning experiences—things like using sand and paper tubes to help students visualize sound vibrations for a lesson on sound waves.

But there was always something missing from this professional learning model: the experience of Robert actually *seeing* me teach. Sure, during our meetings, he saw that I had a solid plan, but did I execute that plan effectively? Were students self-directing their inquiry or merely following directions? How did I really know whether students were learning to apply their new knowledge?

It was reflecting on these types of questions from my own experience that inspired me to create the Edthena video coaching platform. I still sometimes reflect on that difficult first year and imagine how videos of my own teaching for self-reflection and coaching could have amplified the impact Robert was having on my development as a teacher.

Edthena enables teachers to share videos of their classroom teaching so that coaches and colleagues can easily provide timestamped feedback. We work with many different types of education organizations and researchers, and we've collected from them a number of best practices for becoming an organization that uses video evidence to fuel teacher growth and development.

Our hope is that this playbook can help lower the barrier to success for all organizations implementing a video-powered professional learning process.

—Adam

ABOUT THE AUTHORS

Adam Geller is the founder and CEO of Edthena. He started his career in education as a science teacher in St. Louis, Missouri. Since 2011, Adam has overseen the evolution of Edthena from a paper-based prototype into a research-informed and patented platform used by schools, districts, teacher training programs, and professional development providers. Adam has written on education technology topics for various publications including *Education Week*, *Forbes*, and *edSurge*, and he has been an invited speaker about education technology and teacher training for conferences at home and abroad.

Annie Lewis O'Donnell is an independent educational consultant. She works with intentionally diverse school communities that strive to serve all children equitably and with organizations that train and develop teachers. Annie began her career in education as a second-grade teacher at a public school in Baltimore, Maryland. For more than twelve years, she led national design teams at Teach For America, overseeing pre-service teacher preparation and ongoing in-service support.

ABOUT EDTHENA

Edthena is the award-winning classroom observation platform for using teaching videos as part of professional development. Teachers upload classroom videos to share with colleagues who leave time-stamped comments. Edthena also offers specialized collaboration tools to help organizations implement best practices for video-based professional learning. Edthena is the recipient of numerous awards from organizations such as SIIA, *District Administration*, and *Tech & Learning*. For more information, visit http://www.edthena.com. For more news about Edthena, visit http://blog.edthena.com.

PREPARING FOR VIDEO-POWERED PROFESSIONAL LEARNING

CHAPTER 1

TURNING THIS PLAYBOOK INTO A PLAN

Maybe you are already considering using videos of teaching in your professional development plans but feel overwhelmed by how to begin, worried about the limited time you and your teachers have to devote to figuring out a new system. Maybe video coaching already plays a role in developing your teachers, but you suspect it could be more effective. Maybe you're somewhere in between.

Wherever you are, this playbook will help you make and implement a plan for how to best use video-powered professional learning with your teachers. If you're just getting started, this book will help you get up and running quickly and successfully, providing insight into techniques that can be used to deepen the learning teachers get from video-based professional learning. It will also expand your thinking about the types of strategies that can be used with a video platform and the opportunities they afford you and your teachers. But first, it's important to have a clear sense of the goals in mind.

Determine your purpose and choose aligned strategies

This playbook outlines 12 different strategies teachers can use to interact with video evidence of instruction. Which of those 12 you choose to use will depend on your overall goals for teacher professional learning, your teachers' readiness for sharing and viewing videos with one another, and your organization's capacity to plan and support the implementation of these strategies. And while it can be easy to get distracted by all of the interesting and novel ways you might leverage video, it's important that your choices be strategic and purpose-driven.

To choose which strategy or strategies to use, start by first articulating the focus for professional learning. If you weren't using video analysis as a mode for professional learning, what would you want your teachers to be working on in their practice? Are there school-wide goals? Are there areas of focus unique to specific grade-levels or content areas? Or is your professional development program largely differentiated to meet the individual needs of teachers, given their current performance? Consider broader improvement plans in place with your school or district and identify the goals that will unite your professional learning opportunities.

Next, consider your readiness level and that of your teachers and staff. Do your teachers have experience observing one another's class-rooms and collaborating around their work? Or is teaching within your school or district more of a private practice, where individual teachers work to improve behind the closed door of their own class-room? If the latter, you'll need to approach video-based professional learning with caution, as it will represent a significant shift in how your school or district does business. What capacity does your staff have to organize, facilitate, and support these new efforts? If their time or know-how is limited, choose only those strategies that you believe can be done well.

Build a Culture of Trust

Of course, getting the most out of video-based professional learning isn't *quite* as simple as determining a purpose and choosing the right strategies. It's at least as important for your teachers to be comfortable with what might be a new and sometimes scary process.

Putting one's instruction out there for others to view and analyze can be anxiety producing. Indeed, many teachers are hesitant to even watch themselves on video, cringing at what they sound or look like on film, rushing to judge themselves (often quite harshly). Those worries are normal, and the culture you create around video-based professional learning can either ease or exacerbate them. Consider these 10 ideas for building a safe, supportive culture—one where the possible benefits of video-powered learning can be realized.

1. **Be clear that video will be used for professional learning and not for evaluation.**

   Teachers will be more comfortable sharing video publicly if they are certain that it will not be used to evaluate them. To build trust with teachers, communicate clearly that the video they share will only be used to fuel professional learning—to foster growth. Amanda Huza, middle school principal of Equality Charter School in New York City, makes an important point, saying, "The minute the video becomes punitive for teachers, they'll move from authentic engagement in that professional development to compliance with it. And from there, the possibility for learning is limited."

2. **Start small and go slow.**

   At least at the beginning, using video within small groups (i.e., no more than a handful of teachers) can allow individual teachers to build the relationships necessary to make themselves vulnerable—to let their colleagues see them in a light that isn't always the most flattering. In addition to keeping group size small, consider warming teachers up to the idea of sharing video footage by allowing teachers time to practice and gain confidence in new technological skills. It can also help to start with strategies that are lower risk. The first two strategies outlined in the second part of this book—Classroom Tour and Self-Interview—are good starting places to consider. Teachers who are less comfortable with technology may need hands-on support from a colleague when getting started—support that can also contribute to a culture of trust.

3.   **Consider voluntary vs. mandatory participation.**

Some groups, like The Center for the Future of Teaching & Learning (CFTL) at WestEd (2016), advocate for voluntary participation in video-based professional development. Doing so can take a lot of pressure off at the outset. For example, principal Evelyn Cruz tried this approach with a group of teachers in Long Branch, New Jersey, inviting them to a no-obligation presentation. To her surprise, everyone signed up. CFTL also suggests starting a new initiative of this nature with a smaller group of "early adopters." For Evelyn, this meant having participating teachers share with their peers the ways this professional development program helped them grow as practitioners, resulting in a teacher-generated "buzz."

Still others take a different approach, requiring participation as a professional expectation. Though this approach seems more common within pre-service, certification, or residency programs, a school or district leader could also consider it.

4.   **Consider heterogeneous grouping, in terms of experience and proficiency levels.**

Consider how the ways you group teachers for online video analysis can create a culture where everyone, not just one subset of teachers, is improving. In other words, build groups with varied experience—not just early career teachers, and not just veterans. Doing so can show teachers just starting out that, hey, sometimes veterans make mistakes, too. "They backtrack, they problem-solve, they work through challenges," says Debbie Armendariz, Director of Elementary Programs at Portland Public Schools. It can also reinforce the idea that everyone, no matter how senior, always has room to grow.

5. **Sell the benefits of working with video evidence of teaching and learning.**

   Share the reasons why video-based online platforms support teacher growth with staff. For instance, one particular benefit Amanda Huza found persuasive was the way peer videos allow her teachers to see what works and what doesn't with their specific students. She tells teachers, "For all the times you've wondered how something that seems to work so well in that random classroom would go over with your students, now you've got a way to see that."

6. **Celebrate success, growth, and risk-taking.**

   If video is used to foster growth, celebrate when video captures evidence of that growth. Share positive praise. Highlight particularly strong moments in individual videos or across groups. For Amanda Huza, this means making it known when a teacher has done something great. "When I'm talking to a teacher," Amanda says, "I don't let either of us take it for granted that I know about something great in their classroom or about some tremendous growth they've made."

7. **Have leaders model and make themselves vulnerable first.**

   Leaders or facilitators of video coaching should model what they expect of teachers by making themselves vulnerable and reviewing video of their own practice (Knight, 2014). For Megan Kelley-Petersen, director of alternative certification program at the University of Washington, this means having the camera constantly rolling. "And most of the time, it doesn't go as well as

I wish," she says. "I invite [teacher candidates] to wonder with me about choices I made, to help me refine my own practice. In this way, we build a culture of camaraderie around collective improvement."

8. **Use example, instead of exemplar, videos.**

    When offering guidance on the types of video clips to select for analysis and discussion among teachers, researchers advise selecting *examples* rather than *exemplars* (Borko et al., 2010). An exemplar video activates the judgmental side of teacher's brains, which can stymie learning. In fact, because teachers are using these videos to fuel their growth, it's often better to share video that is typical of their everyday practice or demonstrates a challenging area where they'd appreciate support. Professional learning facilitators can also communicate this guidance with teachers directly.

9. **Let teachers drive their professional learning.**

    Empower teachers to capture and view their own video. By doing so, they become active participants in an observation process that has typically rendered them passive. Nancy Jaeger, who directs a teacher residency program in Wisconsin, notes that teachers in her program "have more control over what's being observed by others. They can choose a lesson that highlights where they need help. They have much more flexibility to make observations work for their own improvement than they did when everything was face-to-face."

10. **Create norms around what and how peers comment on video.**

    To create a safe but challenging environment, offer training on and hold people accountable for adhering to clear norms for how they comment on video footage. This might mean asking teachers to refrain from asking questions with an underlying judgment, as Debbie Armendariz does with her teachers. Instead, she asks them to pose questions when they would like to learn more or replicate something they see in a peer's practice. She explains, "This helps teachers avoid veiled critiques. Now, when teachers see comments on their videos, they can assume that peers are questioning because they're hoping to use or learn from your practices." Encourage observers to share specific observations related to learning goals, to ask questions about possible missed opportunities or choices teachers might make in the future, and to steer clear of vague or broad critiques that are disconnected from the evidence or from specific goals.

Giving careful consideration to these ideas and others you generate will help you build the necessary culture to support video-based professional development within your school.

How this playbook is organized

This playbook is organized in two parts. The first part offers guidance as you prepare to use video evidence in professional development. The next chapter opens by outlining the efficacy of evidence-based professional learning, and the following chapter continues with a description of five focusing techniques that help teachers deepen the learning they get from interacting with video evidence of practice.

The second part outlines 12 concrete strategies for online video analysis, one strategy per chapter. Each chapter is structured similarly, opening with a short vignette of the strategy recounting or inspired by that strategy's use in a school. It goes on to elaborate on what the strategy is, describe its benefits and potential impact, and share a step-by-step guide for implementation.

Throughout the playbook, you'll find references to educational researchers whose scholarship supports and has influenced the focusing techniques or the specific professional learning strategies. While this playbook does not provide a comprehensive overview of that research, it does point you in the direction of scholars who have studied topics relevant to this work. We encourage you to seek out the work of these researchers for deeper learning.

CHAPTER 2

PUTTING VIDEO EVIDENCE AT THE CENTER OF PROFESSIONAL LEARNING

Classrooms are complex environments. Most often, the challenges that arise within them are of the adaptive, not just technical, variety. Adaptive challenges can be difficult even to identify, and they have no existing solutions (Heifetz and Linsky, 2008). They require teachers to engage in sustained inquiry to improve their teaching and address unique challenges for students. All of this means that teachers need to be able to learn from their own teaching. As Deborah Ball and David Cohen (1999, p. 10) note, "Much of what [teachers] have to learn must be learned in and from practice, rather than in preparing to practice."

Ball and Cohen imagine professional learning grounded in artifacts that serve as representations of teaching—artifacts like lesson plans, student work samples, and video clips of instruction. Other scholars have echoed this call for practice-based professional development over the years. Pam Grossman, Karen Hammerness, and Morva McDonald (2009), for instance, advocate combining activities that require teachers to practice instruction in classroom settings and simulations like role-plays with those activities that ask them to use concrete artifacts to reflect on their teaching.

In-service teachers often find instructional coaches helpful in supporting them to learn from their daily practice. Bruce Joyce and Beverly Showers (1989) found that ongoing coaching increases teachers' attainment of new instructional skills or strategies as well as increases teachers' consistent and judicious implementation of these new skills with their students. But there are limits to what coaches can provide when they rely solely on in-person observations to offer targeted support.

Because it would be neither practical nor responsible for teachers' learning to happen exclusively in real-time with real students, it is important to structure learning activities around representations of real classroom work (Grossman et al., 2009). Recorded video of classroom instruction is a great representation of this work. And recorded video can also ease the logistical challenges instructional coaches face when they try to observe in-person enough of the right lessons to help teachers improve.

School administrators and instructional coaches play important roles in creating the conditions and offering the support necessary to help teachers learn from their teaching. Through online video analysis, teachers, coaches, and administrators can access and use concrete evidence of teaching and learning to become reflective practitioners who improve their work.

An online video platform can:

- **Give teachers a mirror.**

  Evelyn Cruz, a middle school principal in Long Branch, New Jersey, uses the analogy of video as a mirror in which to examine one's teaching. She tells her teachers, "Every day before we leave home, we look at ourselves in the mirror. We check ourselves. As teachers, video is the way to check our practice in the mirror."

  Indeed, video is a uniquely powerful mirror. Instead of relying on the teacher's memory or notes that an observer took, video serves as an objective record. It can show evidence that the teacher did not see in real-time during instruction. And looking back on video clips can provide the cognitive space teachers need to analyze instruction more productively, because they are not also juggling the pressures of real-time implementation (e.g., the progression of the lesson, the procedures to explain, what students should be doing in-the-moment, etc.).

The ability to annotate video within an online platform allows observers to offer targeted feedback by commenting on specific evidence related to a teacher's learning goals—of exemplary practice or areas to improve. In this way, teachers can learn from very concrete bright spots and from specific aspects of instruction in need of improvement. And because the video and related commentary are archived online, teachers can look back and examine growth over time.

Research supports the benefits of teachers watching videos of their classrooms. Studies have shown that teachers are motivated to learn from their own instructional videos and feel their learning is more significant and meaningful as compared to what they gain by viewing video clips of other teachers (Seidel et al., 2011). Other research has documented positive instructional changes as a result of teachers' work with video evidence, including improved question-asking strategies, increased time for students to share and comment on each other's work, and shifts from providing general positive statements to specific positive feedback to students (Tripp and Rich, 2012).

- **Help build instructional communities.**
  Powerful learning is possible when teachers work in networks that make viewing peer video a central activity. Several studies have found that teachers' participation in such professional learning communities helped them to build vital professional knowledge and improve their practice—particularly around

what they noticed within instructional videos and discussed with their peers (Little, 2002; Sherin and Han, 2004).

- **Help teachers see themselves as their students do.**
  John Hattie's Visible Learning (2008) argues that teachers need to be able to see learning in their classrooms through the eyes of their students. Once they have, they can better evaluate their own teaching; they can understand its effects on student learning and determine how to improve. Video provides a mechanism for teachers to see directly how their teaching is having an impact on student participation and learning.

An online video platform also offers additional advantages to peers, coaches, administrators, and supervisors, including:

- allowing the appropriate people to be available at the appropriate time to view the appropriate moments of classroom instruction;
- easing logistical challenges related to scheduling in-person observations, securing coverage for teachers to observe one another, etc.;
- reducing travel time for observers across geography (e.g., rural areas, large metro areas, statewide programs);
- providing coaches, administrators, and supervisors with concrete evidence of what teachers are able to do as a result of coaching, professional development, or training; and
- producing videos that can be used in future professional learning opportunities.

Putting video evidence at the center of a systematic approach to teacher professional development is wise, but is no silver bullet for improving teaching and learning in schools.

Like any new initiative, its success depends on doing the work of planning logistics, developing a smart strategy, establishing a supportive culture, and then implementing it well, day-in and day-out. The following chapters can guide you in doing the necessary work to make video-powered professional learning successful for your school or organization.

CHAPTER 3

FOCUSING TECHNIQUES FOR INTERACTING WITH VIDEO EVIDENCE

The majority of this book shares ideas for how to structure and implement video-powered professional learning strategies. However, it's also helpful to name and define the different and particular ways that educators will analyze the evidence they collect. Productive analysis consists of more than simply watching videos and leaving comments on what you observe.

The following five focusing techniques can help teachers, coaches, teacher educators, and administrators more skillfully interact with video evidence, improve their ability to reflect, and drive their own professional growth.

The Five Focusing Techniques

For our purposes, we're using the term "focusing techniques" to describe helpful ways of working with the video evidence you obtain and review. These techniques are synthesized from research about deepening teacher learning, promoting self-reflection, and accelerating improvement.

SPOT

What makes an aspect of instruction meaningful varies. A moment might be important because it illustrates cause and effect relationships in the classroom. It might be meaningful because it is surprising and different from what the teacher expected. Or, it might be of note because it illustrates a principle of teaching and learning on which a school has been working. **Spot** helps teachers discern a moment, an interaction, or a pattern of behavior as meaningful.

For example, where a teacher places the homework return folder may not be important in and of itself. However, if you're examining classroom procedures, and the particular placement of that folder in some way contributes to a change in classroom efficiency, it becomes important. Teachers may Spot other seemingly small things, like the proximity of teachers to students during lessons, as important to the quality of their relationships with students or the focus and concentration they support students to maintain.

Spot is a particularly helpful focusing technique for teachers building video analysis skills. Help teachers deepen their skill with this technique by connecting what they see in recorded evidence to qualities of teaching that they've identified as important as well as why they are important. For example, a teacher might Spot the moment when an early childhood teacher kneels down to eye-level with a pre-K student to correct a behavior. The teacher might call the interaction notable because being on eye-level helps teachers gain the full attention of and build connected relationships with children. Press the teacher to explain why this kind of secure, attached relationship matters so much in early childhood. Then, rewatch the footage to Spot additional examples of teacher moves that help build such relationships.

BREAK DOWN

Break Down supports teachers to break teaching and learning down into component parts. It requires us to identify smaller pieces of a larger practice, attach a name to and describe each piece, and explain how each piece relates to the whole. Having recorded evidence of instruction allows you to break down the work of teaching very specifically.

For example, you might break down clips of students discussing a novel into component parts, like identifying literary devices and analyzing them to determine an author's intended meaning. Or, you might examine a video to break down the instructional methods that help students uncover the novel's meaning, such as chunking the text into meaningful sections, using interactive read alouds to scaffold student thinking, and modeling how to make and support claims with textual evidence. Any one of those pedagogies can be broken down even further into more specific teaching moves, helping make the daunting task of supporting students to analyze text more manageable for teachers.

Break Down is particularly helpful for teachers adopting new instructional practices. Similar to learning to swing a bat—a skill that involves practicing the set-up, the grip, the swing, and the follow-through—Break Down turns a complex pedagogical activity into a series of steps—steps that can be practiced discreetly until they become an automatic and unified habit. Once this habit is established, teachers have cognitive energy available to adapt the pedagogy to best meet the observed needs of students.

INTERPRET

Where Spot and Break Down focus on finding moments of interest and breaking them into constituent parts, **Interpret** focuses the observer on determining the underlying causes of these moments. This interpretation can happen at a more surface, but still significant, level. For example, an observer might note a question the teacher posed to elicit student thinking about equivalent fractions, identify the resulting evidence of student thinking, and analyze why the question did or didn't work in that case.

Interpret can also happen at a deeper level—one that calls for a teacher's personal introspection. A teacher might observe a pattern of posing rigorous academic questions to one subset of students less frequently than she poses them to others and decide to examine that pattern. The teacher might unearth underlying assumptions made about certain students and try to determine what shaped those assumptions. The teacher might seek evidence to confirm or revise those assumptions, compare those assumptions to his or her underlying values, or try to determine how those assumptions might influence his or her behavior.

In this way, teachers can progress from watching the effects between teacher, students, and the environment to make sense of classroom events by using what they know of the real people involved and their underlying beliefs, motivations, and assumptions. This is the work of Interpret.

Being able to interpret the underlying causes behind spotted events is a critical analytical skill for teachers to develop if they are to accelerate their own professional learning. It is important that teachers can drive their own learning, because regardless of the quality of pre-service preparation, or the volume and effectiveness of in-service development, the relational and evolving nature of the teaching profession requires teachers to constantly improve. Being able to determine why things are happening as they are in the classroom is key to unlocking that constant improvement.

COMPARE

The three focusing techniques described so far can be used with one discrete piece of video evidence. The fourth technique, **Compare,** can be used to distinguish the similarities and differences between two or more pieces of evidence. This most often means comparing two moments in time, but it can also mean comparing two representations of the same event.

The multiple pieces of evidence you or your teachers might select depends on your purpose. For example, it might be helpful to compare different moments from within the same video, or to compare a video of instruction with its accompanying lesson plan or resulting evidence of student learning. Or, it might be useful to compare videos of several teachers' instruction of the same course material or of their interactions with the same group of students.

Regardless of what evidence teachers are comparing, the power for professional learning comes from having at least two concrete artifacts of teaching and learning, two moments in time within the same artifact, or two representations of the same event that are in some way related to one another. Teachers sharpen their judgment and fuel their motivation to change as they tease out the cause and effect relationships between the two artifacts, moments, or representations.

DISCUSS

Though the previous four focusing techniques can be used independently by an educator as he or she examines recorded evidence of practice, the techniques are often more effective when used collaboratively with peers and coaches. **Discuss** is a technique that involves analyzing aspects of teaching with others, in order to elicit, understand, and consider others' perspectives and ideas. Choosing to utilize the Discuss technique is the purposeful shift from "getting feedback about my teaching" to "talking together about teaching."

Discuss is particularly useful when teachers are interpreting or comparing evidence of teaching. Through discussion, other people can pose questions, suggest alternative interpretations, or probe the thought process to strengthen the teacher's thinking. Sometimes, discussion acts to affirm a teacher's thinking and can build confidence. Other times, discussion can help the teacher uncover often unconscious thought processes—processes that can be difficult to surface independently.

Discuss can happen asynchronously as online threaded comments, synchronously via video conference or in-person meeting, or a blend of both. Each mode of discussion encourages a deeper analysis of the evidence. For example, asynchronous discussion may afford participants the amount of "think time" they need, which differs between people. Synchronous discussion may offer access to additional information like body language or create the opportunity to respond more readily. Discussion facilitators may benefit from consulting the framework for facilitating video-based professional development, developed by Elizabeth van Es et al. (2014) and reprinted in the appendix of this playbook.

Supporting Teachers to Use Focusing Techniques

As you read the second part of this playbook, you'll see the focusing techniques referenced as ways to interact with video evidence in the context of specific learning strategies. But the focusing techniques themselves need to be learned and adopted by educators.

Educators who are new to examining video evidence may grapple with which aspects of instruction are important for analysis. After all, there is much about the classroom environment, the teacher, the students, and the interactions among all three to observe. Be on the lookout for the tendency to largely watch and describe teacher actions. Over time, push observers to note the effects of teacher actions on student learning and well-being.

Additionally, helping observers to discern cause and effect requires them to build their interpretive skills. Novice observers may find it overwhelming to interpret why events and interactions are happening as they are. Productive interactions between teacher and student can seem almost magical, while the causes of challenges can seem impossible to untangle. When getting started with video observations, it's challenging to discern what matters most, to interpret the underlying causes of classroom events, and to elicit and consider the perspectives of others.

You can help others to use these techniques with increasing effectiveness by:

- modeling how to pick and apply a focusing technique;
- making transparent your thought-process and rationale;
- leveraging frameworks or rubrics as common language to describe the practices of teaching;
- inviting others to react by clarifying, challenging, or extending your models or rationale;
- gradually releasing responsibility for using the techniques;
- responding to others' use of techniques and justifying thinking;
- offering reflection questions, protocols, or tools to support teachers' use of the techniques; and
- encouraging others to solicit and consider additional perspectives on evidence.

Research that supports the focusing techniques

The ideas in this chapter represent an interpretation of a strong body of research about teacher learning from video evidence. If you'd like to further your investigation into the underlying research that supports these five focusing techniques, we suggest a few jumping-off points:

- Miriam Sherin and Elizabeth van Es's work around teacher noticing and teachers' professional vision;
- Elizabeth van Es and colleagues' work on facilitating teachers' analysis of videos;
- Pam Grossman and colleagues' work on the decomposition of teacher practice; and
- Rossella Santagata, Hilda Borko, Judy Jacobs, and colleagues' work on using video for teacher training.

VIDEO-POWERED PROFESSIONAL LEARNING STRATEGIES

S T R A T E G Y   1

CLASSROOM TOUR

Kaleigh O'Donnell is a fifth-grade teacher at Westlawn Elementary School in Fairfax County, Virginia. At the beginning of the year, Kaleigh records a less-than-five-minute video in which she describes the way she's organized her classroom. At the beginning of the tour, Kaleigh takes several wide-angle videos of the way she's set-up classroom community supplies, highlights what's hanging on the walls at the start of the school year, and shows how she arranges and stores books for literature circles.

The bulk of Kaleigh's video tour focuses on how she's organized the central learning spaces in her room. She shows and describes her two whole-group meeting areas—one where all students can gather on a large carpet in front of the smart board and another in the classroom library. Next, she moves to a small group meeting area where students can work with one another. She explains that she's placed this meeting area in a corner of the room to give students a quiet space to work with one another, and has hung productive talk prompts on the wall to support discussion. Finally, Kaleigh shows how she's arranged student desks in small groups to facilitate dialogue.

Kaleigh shares her classroom tour with a coach and a group of peers in her master's cohort, so that they have a sense of what her physical space looks like and why she's arranged it in this way before they view clips of lessons.

What is Classroom Tour?

In **Classroom Tour**, teachers capture and upload a short video showing the organization of their classroom and the systems in place, explaining the thinking underlying the classroom's structure. In other words, teachers narrate a walk-through of their empty classroom or workspace, highlighting why and how the physical space and materials are organized to support student learning. They then share footage with peers and coaches either for immediate feedback or as a window into the design of a classroom those partners will observe across the year.

Teachers might choose to show and explain any or all aspects of their classroom environment, including the overall layout and aesthetics, what's displayed on the walls, how various learning spaces are organized, where and how student and teacher materials are organized, how work and messages going home and returning to school are stored, and so on. These choices could reflect where the teacher needs support, feels most proud of, or what a peer or coach has asked them to focus on in the tour.

When reviewing classroom tours, teachers can spot meaningful organizational choices. They can compare systems planned for different parts of the room or different class periods, as well as the organizational decisions different teachers make. Perhaps, most importantly, they can identify specific, concrete ideas to borrow for use in their own classroom environments.

What are the benefits and impact of Classroom Tour?

Classroom tours provide insight into a teacher's classroom or workspace setup, allowing educators to exchange ideas and learn from each other. Tours can also provide important context for those who cannot visit in-person but will be supporting the teacher across the year.

Implementing a Classroom Tour as one of the first video observation experiences for a teacher is a gentle, productive way to get teachers started with a new process. Classroom tours can help teachers build confidence using the technology required to capture, upload, and share video. Looking at classroom spaces and sharing positive expectations for what will happen in that space during the school year can limit risk for teachers. Getting teachers comfortable with the idea of using videos and building confidence with the technology are important steps in rolling out video-powered learning.

How do you implement Classroom Tour?

PLANNING

- **Guide teachers to narrate and capture a short, two- to five-minute tour of their empty classroom.**
  Ask teachers to highlight the various learning spaces and explain why the room is arranged as it is. It is not necessary nor even recommended for the teacher to appear on camera as part of the tour.

  Beyond those guidelines, determine how directive to be in terms of what teachers should include in their Classroom Tour. At the more directive end of the spectrum, ask teachers to focus their tour on particular classroom design choices that reflect something they've learned about or are trying to improve, like how space might nurture focus and concentration, how desk layout might support dialogue, or how wall hangings might serve to bring students' home lives or cultures into the classroom. Alternatively, leave the choice of what to feature in Classroom Tour entirely up to teacher discretion. Though there are good reasons to be more or less directive in guidance to teachers, if this strategy is an introduction to video coaching, it should be as unintimidating as possible.

  Plan to spend about 10 minutes sharing guidance with teachers about the structure and necessary components of the classroom tour. Allow another 5 minutes for teachers to consider that guidance and decide what to feature in the tour.

EXECUTION

- **Teachers capture the Classroom Tour.**

  Teachers should plan to spend two to five minutes narrating and capturing their tours.

- **Teachers share video for others to view.**

  Teachers can choose whether to pose specific questions or requests to peers and coaches who will view the video. Those observers can then respond to specific queries or offer general reactions or feedback. Observers should plan to spend equal to the total run-time of the footage to view and share comments on each video.

In total, Classroom Tour can happen over one or several days. Planning for the learning strategy takes 10 minutes for observers and five minutes for the classroom teachers determining what to capture. Implementing Classroom Tour takes the teacher two to five minutes. Viewing and analyzing the footage takes about five minutes.

SELF-INTERVIEW

As part of professional development in the week before students arrive for the start of the new school year, teachers at Greenwood Elementary School record themselves describing their goals for students in the upcoming school year. They consider state standards, end-of-year exams, the socioemotional skills their school has targeted, the admission requirements for a select middle school program many students want to attend, and input from families and students themselves. Using a few mock interview questions as a guide, teachers create a five-minute video explaining these goals and why they matter.

After uploading the video, each teacher shares it with one colleague from the grade-level below and the grade-level above, inviting feedback. In this way, teachers across the school can draw inspiration from their colleagues' thinking and check the vertical alignment of expectations for students across grade-levels at the school.

What is Self-Interview?

Self-Interview involves a teacher recording a video describing his or her goals for individual students, an entire class, or their own professional growth. In Self-Interview, teachers describe and offer rationale for goals they have set for students—say, why those goals matter to student learning and well-being—or for their own professional growth, capture this description on video, and share the clip with peers and coaches for feedback. This strategy is used to prompt teacher thinking, to generate insight from others, and to frame the overall purpose of the classroom as a learning environment that peers and coaches will observe across the year.

Self-Interview can help support teachers to become what Donald Schon (1983) called self-reflective practitioners—professional educators whose instruction is informed by continuously developing judgment about what students should achieve, what they need, and the contexts in which students are growing and learning. It is important to examine teacher thinking in addition to and alongside concrete evidence of teacher and student actions; recording and sharing some of that judgment makes this possible.

What are the benefits and impact of Self-Interview?

Particularly when completed early in a teacher's experience with video observations, Self-Interview helps peers and coaches build important context for the instruction they will observe, allows an exchange of ideas and best practices, and builds initial experience and confidence with technology and with examining video evidence.

In addition, Self-Interview affords teachers the opportunity to access the thought processes and inspirations of a peer, so they might refine or adjust their own goals for students or themselves. Capturing Self-Interview on video also creates an important artifact for future reflection, as a point of comparison with recorded evidence of their actions in the classroom. In this way, teachers can consider how well their daily interactions are aligned with their larger goals for students or how far they have progressed toward a personal self-improvement goal.

As an example of how Self-Interview might support future reflection, researchers Lynn Bryan and Art Recesso (2006) asked secondary science student teachers to document what they considered to be great science teaching and learning. Over the course of the semester, teachers compared video evidence of their instruction with their recorded belief statements. Examining their actual practice helped the teachers spot some segments of instruction that demonstrated alignment between belief and practice and others that lacked alignment. The teachers could then work to interpret the underlying causes in each case.

Bryan and Recesso concluded that when teachers are able to see examples of their beliefs in action in the classroom, they build confidence in their decision-making skills. Conversely, when they spot the opposite, they can bring focus to their professional learning, productively engaging professors and peers in weighing and selecting alternative instructional approaches that might better align with their aspirations.

How do you implement Self-Interview?

PLANNING

- **Give teachers parameters.**
  Consider offering a high-level prompt or creating mock interview questions to support teacher thinking. Plan to spend about 10 minutes sharing this guidance with teachers.

EXECUTION

- **Teachers record a video describing their goals for individual students, whole classes, or their own professional learning.**
  Teachers should plan to spend about ten minutes preparing for and another five minutes capturing the Self-Interview.

- **Teachers share the video with colleagues.**
  Because Self-Interview offers important context for those who will view classroom footage throughout the year, it is helpful to share with all people who will observe the classroom.

- **Peers and coaches view and consider Self-Interview footage.**
  Others can spot meaningful moments in the teacher's explanation and offer reactions and thoughts. These can be affirming, clarifying, or probing. The teacher and his or her peers and coaches might engage in asynchronous discussion about this feedback, or the recorded teacher might mull the feedback independently or with a coach. Those viewing Self-Interview footage should plan to spend at least as long as the total run time of the clip for review.

In total, Self-Interview can happen over one or several days. To plan the learning strategy, budget about 10 minutes. To implement Self-Interview, plan for the teacher to spend 15 minutes and observers to spend 5-10 minutes.

STRATEGY 3

EXAMPLE ANALYSIS

Crystal McMachen teaches middle school math and serves as a virtual mentor to another teacher in her home state of South Dakota. Crystal's mentee, Stacy Cope, works in a school with only two math teachers. In order to develop Stacy's skills for questioning strategies, Crystal records herself teaching and shares the clip with Stacy.

Both teachers analyze Crystal's clip to break down the lesson and spot questions that helped students share their problem-solving strategies and consider alternative ones. They discuss their ideas asynchronously through comments on the video.

What is Example Analysis?

In **Example Analysis**, teachers view and analyze a video artifact of teaching relevant to their specific learning goals, deepening their understanding of what constitutes quality teaching and learning, so that they might apply that knowledge within their own practice. The video is selected by the person guiding a given teacher or teachers' development. For example, a coach may select a video of a different teacher in the school implementing a specific pedagogical technique. Similarly, a professional developer may share a clip from an adopted curriculum publisher to help teachers across a school district deepen their understanding of how to implement that curriculum.

The specific types of analyses teachers do depends on their professional learning goals. Teachers might spot particular moments of importance within a clip, break down the instructional practice they view into component parts, or interpret cause-and-effect relationships at play in the instruction. They can then discuss their ideas with other educators. To maximize learning, it helps to prompt teachers to use relevant specific focusing techniques as they interact with chosen examples.

Example Analysis is influenced by Video Grand Rounds (VGRs), developed at Eastern Carolina University (Cuthrell et al., 2016). Elementary education faculty use VGRs as a substitute for the earliest in-field observations, which previously happened in classrooms across the local community. Instead of traveling to these schools, teacher candidates view four faculty-selected video examples, use a standardized observation guide to structure their analysis, and engage in a debrief discussion with peers and faculty.

What are the benefits and impact of Example Analysis?

Example Analysis affords several benefits to educators. At a basic level, example videos can show teachers how to implement a particular lesson, instructional strategy, or curriculum. Teachers can watch and rewatch an example to help them prepare to implement a new practice with their own students.

Analysis of example video also helps sharpen teachers' abilities to spot meaningful aspects of instruction and to recognize the full complexity of classroom interactions (Cuthrell et al., 2016). It has been shown to change what teachers think about and discuss with peers and coaches, turning their attention from teacher performance to the nature of student thinking (Borko et al., 2010).

Additionally, teachers who begin examining more deeply their students' thinking through Example Analysis actually improve their ability to respond to student thinking in action in their classrooms (Cohen, 2004). Most importantly, as teachers build their skill with Example Analysis, their students learn more (Kersting et al., 2009).

Example Analysis is an approach to professional development that is scalable across a district or network, allows for high degrees of quality control over the content, and is more personalized and in-depth than a traditional sit-and-get demonstration of a pedagogical strategy would be.

How do you implement Example Analysis?

PLANNING

- **Select an example video clip for analysis.**
  Video clips can be chosen from those teachers have previously uploaded (with permission), can be pulled from an external video library, or can feature a professional developer or facilitator modeling a pedagogical strategy. These clips can be set either in a role-play or in-context with students.

  The footage selected should illustrate some aspect of instruction that aligns with teachers' goals. Depending on those goals, choose an example or a nonexample of a desired practice. Watching examples can help teachers identify practices to emulate. Nonexamples—examples of realistic mistakes—can help teachers identify common pitfalls to avoid. Consider clips that demonstrate common challenges in teacher practice or common misconceptions in student thinking.

The length of a chosen clip can vary. Shorter clips can be valuable if teachers are trying to break down a specific pedagogical strategy or work on a small component of their instruction, like the clarity of their directions for student work. Longer videos help teachers see how teaching and learning evolves across a lesson, which is often challenging to see in real-time. For instance, analyzing a longer clip can be valuable if teachers are striving to determine moments of importance or to prepare to implement complete lessons from a new curriculum.

Those people selecting example videos should plan to spend about 30 minutes on this step.

- **Share selected video examples and guidance for teachers' analysis.**
  Share your selected video clip with teachers for independent analysis, which can remain unstructured by simply asking educators to analyze and determine moments of importance. The benefit of unstructured analysis is that it can serve to check an educator's understanding. For example, when training teachers to observe one another, unguided analysis serves as a good way to ensure everyone shares a common vision for instruction.

  Alternatively, provide more structure by asking teachers to ground their analysis in a shared framework or by preparing guiding questions. Develop questions that require teachers to spot evidence of student thinking and the teacher moves that enabled it and to rationalize their thinking.

  Those people structuring teachers' analysis of example videos should plan to spend about 15 minutes on this step.

- **Decide whether to include discussion.**
  Discussion of Example Analysis is optional and can happen synchronously or asynchronously. If teachers engage in discussion, consider focusing on areas of agreement or disagreement. The former allows teachers to build upon and strengthen one another's ideas, while the latter allows them to surface and consider their colleagues' rationale. Plan to spend 15 minutes preparing to facilitate.

EXECUTION

- **Teachers view and analyze example video clips.**
  Teachers use provided guidance to analyze the example, annotating the evidence they've spotted as important within the clip. Teachers should plan to spend roughly one-and-a-half times the total run time of the example video to view and analyze the footage.

- **Those in charge of teacher development examine teachers' analysis.**
  Whether a professional developer, coach, or administrator, those in charge of a teacher's development examine the ways that he or she has analyzed the example. This might happen by responding to the teacher's annotated comments to affirm, push, or raise alternative interpretations for the teacher to consider. Or, if discussion is planned, simply make note of topics to raise to offer feedback on the strength of teacher analyses. Plan to spend roughly one-and-a-half times the total runtime of the example video to read and consider each teacher's analysis.

- **If chosen, teachers engage in discussion about the analysis.**
  Teachers should plan to spend 30 minutes if a discussion is included in this learning strategy.

Example Analysis can happen over several days or weeks. Those planning the learning strategy should plan to spend an hour on that work. In the execution phase, teachers should plan to spend 20-50 minutes, depending on the runtime of the selected video example. Those planning Example Analysis should budget approximately fifteen minutes to consider each teacher's analysis and an additional 30 minutes if engaging in discussion.

STRATEGY 4

PRE-TEACH

As teacher educators who specialize in elementary math at University of Michigan, Meghan Shaughnessy and Susanna Farmer want to ensure their teacher interns can correctly explain and model the complex idea of multiplying fractions to their elementary school students. The week before implementing a lesson on this topic in their internship classroom, Meghan and Susanna ask their teachers to record approximately 90-seconds of video of themselves explaining, as if to a fifth-grader, how to use an area-model representation to solve a fraction multiplication problem. They guide their teachers to capture the actual example they plan to use with students during instruction.

Meghan and Susanna review the videos and provide comments on strengths and things each teacher might consider changing before the teacher delivers the lesson later in the week. In total, Meghan and Susanna spend less than 10 minutes on each teacher, gaining a clear sense of what the intern is prepared to do while also offering targeted and meaningful feedback on core aspects of instruction. As teachers finish preparing to teach, they request clarification on specific comments when necessary.

What is Pre-Teach?

Pre-Teach involves teachers recording themselves rehearsing portions of upcoming instruction in order to refine their practice before implementing with students. Videos can be as short as 90 seconds or upward of five to seven minutes. Pre-Teach is meant to approximate real teaching practice and can be implemented with or without others role-playing as students. Pre-Teach is a powerful strategy since it helps teachers practice and make adjustments *before* their lessons rather than analyze teaching that has happened in the past.

Pre-Teach helps teachers prepare for the delivery, not just the design, of lessons. Since it requires teachers to try out the particulars of a lesson—the particular image they might show, the particular questions they might pose, or the particular language they might use to describe a phenomena, for example—this strategy functions as an important intermediate step between planning a lesson and implementing it. Teachers might consider pre-teaching episodes of instruction that will require them to help students engage in discourse, elicit and respond to students' ideas, communicate core content, organize instructional materials, navigate social and intellectual relationships among students, and so forth.

Pre-Teach is an evolution of the microteaching practice developed in the 1960s by Dwight Allen and colleagues at Stanford University. Microteaching involves teacher candidates teaching short segments of lessons to small groups of students, receiving feedback from students and observers, considering how to adjust based on that feedback, and reteaching that same short lesson to a new group of students. While microteaching and video-recorded rehearsals have since become popular within teacher training programs, here they are adapted into a format appropriate for both pre-service and in-service teachers.

Pre-Teach can happen in two formats: solo and with peers. A solo Pre-Teach happens with only one teacher and his or her recording device. In this version, the teacher can focus on trying out sequences such as key explanations, demonstrations, or directions to give to students.

Alternatively, Pre-Teach can happen with peers or coaches who role play students while one teacher practices. This version allows the teacher doing the Pre-Teach to try out episodes of instruction that require sustained interaction, like eliciting and responding to students or supporting students to engage deeply with the content of the lesson.

When Pre-Teach videos are shared, teachers can invite peers and coaches to spot moments of importance and offer specific feedback, as well as support them in breaking down or interpreting their Pre-Teach performance. Using these focusing techniques to analyze the Pre-Teach video can help teachers refine their instruction before they implement with students. Teachers who view a peer's rehearsal video can also gain new insight for their own instruction.

What are the benefits and impact of Pre-Teach?

Many video learning strategies focus on instruction that has already occurred with students. Pre-Teach is one of the few strategies that can improve instruction before it occurs with students.

All teachers, early-career and experienced, can benefit from implementing Pre-Teach for techniques and content they're delivering for the first time or working to refine. In fact, a recent study by Francis John Troyan and Megan Madigan Peercy (2016) found that teachers see these types of rehearsals as important to their own preparation.

While the solo version of Pre-Teach is logistically simple to implement and highly valuable to the teacher involved, it doesn't afford the opportunity for teachers try out segments of instruction that rely on significant interactions with students. To compensate, teachers can pause themselves during the Pre-Teach, momentarily step out of the role of teacher, and talk through what they expect their students to do or say.

The role-play version of Pre-Teach offers the opportunity to prepare for interactions with and between students. However, this benefit comes with its own set of drawbacks. Teachers can find it awkward to play a student, potentially distracting the rehearsing teacher from the task at hand. Establishing clear norms for role play—like asking teachers to respond with the ideas they most commonly hear from their own students, follow directions, and demonstrate good behavior—can help mitigate this challenge.

Simply to coordinate everyone involved, implementing Pre-Teach with role plays also requires more directive facilitation from a coach or teacher educator. This kind of heavy direction may be less desirable for the professional development of more experienced teachers.

Regardless of the format used, when teachers record and share Pre-Teach clips, colleagues and coaches can offer feedback equally or even more effectively than they could if a written lesson plan was the only artifact of preparation. A recorded Pre-Teach allows a coach to understand much more clearly and directly how a teacher plans to represent ideas for students, compared to what they can infer from reading the teacher's lesson plan.

For example, Meghan Shaughnessy noted in the first five seconds of one Pre-Teach video that the teacher changed a math problem from asking students to find "three-fifths of two-thirds" to asking them to find "one-half of one-half." Meghan could foresee the confusion these specific fractions might cause as students tried to use the teacher's area-model representation to solve the fraction multiplication problem. She left a brief comment, asking the teacher to reconsider the numbers in the problem to avoid confusion when introducing the concept to students. In this way, the teacher benefited from quick, actionable feedback before she taught the lesson to students.

Pre-Teach video clips also make the process of giving and receiving feedback on the instructional plan much more efficient. Teachers have to spend less time writing out detailed explanations just to make their plans clear to a feedback provider. Those providing feedback spend less time trying to discern what the lesson author intends because they can literally see what the teacher is prepared to do.

How do you implement Pre-Teach?

PLANNING

- **Decide what teachers should capture.**
  One clear guideline is that Pre-Teach is reserved for *upcoming* lessons, so teachers can prepare intellectually and logistically. Beyond that, teachers can benefit from Pre-Teaching a variety of segments of instruction.

  Those new to teaching might decide to Pre-Teach parts of instruction that help them build initial comfort with the language and representations of the discipline, the necessary clarity of explanations, or the specificity of student directions. Those more familiar may Pre-Teach a particularly challenging segment for feedback before implementing the lesson.

  Consider whether to be prescriptive about what teachers Pre-Teach or to leave the choice entirely to the teacher. Regardless, make your expectations clear. Plan to spend five minutes making this decision.

- **Choose the solo or role-play version of the strategy.**
  Considering the benefits and drawbacks, plan to spend about five minutes deciding which version of the strategy teachers should use.

EXECUTION

- **Teachers capture a Pre-Teach and share online.**
  Once the parameters for Pre-Teach are established, teachers implement and capture it and then share on the video platform.

  If using the solo version of the strategy, plan to spend about 10 minutes for teachers to prepare, record, and share their Pre-Teach clip. If using the role-play version, plan to spend about 20 minutes for teachers to prepare, record, and share; 15 minutes for role-playing educators to participate; and 20 minutes for the facilitator to coordinate and direct the role-play.

- **Analyze and discuss the Pre-Teach.**
Use a school's rubrics, framework, or performance criteria and the Spot, Break Down, and Interpret focusing techniques to help everyone viewing the Pre-Teach to structure their analyses.

  If a group of teachers is analyzing a peer's Pre-Teach clip, let teachers leave and respond to one another's comments asynchronously. Or, facilitate a synchronous discussion for educators to view and discuss the clip at the same time.

  Those viewing Pre-Teach clips should plan to spend one-and-a-half times the total runtime of the video clip to analyze and discuss asynchronously. If having a synchronous discussion, budget an additional 20 minutes.

In total, Pre-Teach can happen over one or several days. The planning work should only take 10 minutes. In execution, teachers should plan to spend between 10-20 minutes recording their Pre-Teach videos. If the role-play version of Pre-Teach is used, educators who role-play students should plan to spend an additional 15 minutes, while the person coordinating the role-play should plan for an additional 20 minutes. Educators analyzing and discussing Pre-Teach videos should budget 10-30 minutes.

VIDEO OBSERVATION

A sixth-grade math teacher shares with his instructional coach, David Baker of St. Vrain Valley Schools, that he's worried about classroom management. He is not sure what's causing the continual challenges he experiences with his post-lunch class period. He is feeling immense pressure from his principal, who is very worried about the learning time students lose in such a chaotic environment. David has the teacher record and share a clip of this particular class to view together.

The footage is challenging for the teacher to watch. It takes a full 13 minutes for students to enter the room and settle down enough to hear directions and instruction. Even after that length of time, students are quiet but not working on math. The teacher watches as a student dawdling along the back edge of the room repeatedly opens and closes locker doors. The teacher is shocked, as he had not even seen this happen in real-time. The teacher stops the video, says he can't watch anymore, and tells David that something has to change and change quickly. He can no longer allow so much instructional time to be wasted and so much disorder to take hold.

David capitalizes on the teacher's resolve by asking him to describe how he would like the classroom to function differently. The teacher is quite clear. He wants students to enter, greet him personally, and efficiently begin a silent, independent math task to open the lesson. Together, they outline a set of tight procedures to help students transition quickly from lunch to math. They then make a plan for teaching those procedures to students.

A week later, the teacher shares footage of this same class. In one week, students have reduced the time it takes to get focused and working from 13 minutes to less than 3 minutes. David asks the teacher if he's satisfied with this change. The teacher believes the class can get focused in less than a minute. In two more weeks, when they look at another clip, students in this class take under 30 seconds to enter and begin the math lesson. The teacher shares that his principal is now calling this class a model for how to maximize instructional time and wants to share a video of students implementing the transition procedures with other teachers in the building.

What is Video Observation?

Video Observation is the learning strategy that many imagine when they talk about implementing video-powered professional learning. In essence, it moves the standard classroom observation to a virtual platform. Through capturing and sharing footage of their class in progress, teachers can work on their own or with partners to determine the current state of teaching and learning and identify next steps to support continued professional growth.

Traditionally, classroom observations involve an observer sitting in the back of a classroom and watching what happens, often taking notes to be analyzed and shared with the teacher at a later time. With Video Observation, the teacher and other observers can see and analyze all or part of a lesson from the same perspective and with the added ability to pause to think or rewind to take a second look. Video Observation allows the teacher to take stock of their classroom to determine what to do next, independently or with help from others.

To support their reflection, teachers use any or all of the focusing techniques described in chapter 3 to interact with their video evidence and note comments within the clips, including affirmations and areas for improvement. An observation partner highlights both practices to extend into future instruction and those to adjust, based on how those practices impact students. An observer can share feedback in reference to a framework or rubric that the school uses to align around common expectations and aspirations for students and teachers.

In addition to feedback, teachers and other observers can suggest specific learning strategies to drive professional development, including those outlined within this playbook. For example, teachers working to improve student discourse might benefit from engaging in Example Analysis of another classroom's student discussion and then implementing Pre-Teach for the set-up to an upcoming discussion for input.

Video Observation plays a unique role in this playbook as a pivot point of sorts, marking an increase in strategy complexity as teachers begin to capture and deeply examine their own teaching. This learning strategy, combined with strategies covered earlier, sets the stage for many of the more advanced strategies shared in the remainder of the text.

What are the benefits and impact of Video Observation?

Given the complexity of teaching, and both the performative and relational aspects of the work entailed, it stands to reason that meaningful continuous improvement cannot happen without close examination of evidence of practice. But the case for observing and sharing feedback with teachers extends beyond common sense. Research studies (including Elish-Piper and L'Allier, 2011; Allen et al., 2011) have concluded that observing and giving teachers accurate and actionable feedback also boosts student achievement.

A key benefit of Video Observation compared to an in-person observation is that it offers more opportunities for teachers to actively participate in their own improvement. In reflecting on the sixth-grade math teacher who tightened up his transition procedures, David Baker explains:

In a traditional coaching cycle, this teacher wouldn't have had the visceral experience of having to sit through 13 minutes of unfocused disruption. He wouldn't have had to squirm as he watched a student opening lockers at the back of the classroom. Because we are both watching the footage, the teacher doesn't have to rely on me to tell him that happened in his room. He doesn't just read my notes. He sees it for himself. And seeing it for himself is a very gut-level experience. It motivates him to make big changes. And then, after he implements changes in his practice, he can see the difference in his students for himself. That is empowering.

Amanda Huza, a middle school principal, echoes this sentiment:

> I believe that online classroom observations can level the play-ing field between teachers and administrators. When teachers can watch themselves and their peers, they have the same per-spective as the observer. The evidence is visible to both people, and they can discuss it on equal footing. Without that video evidence, teachers are at a disadvantage because they don't have the luxury of sitting back and viewing all that happens in a classroom. Online observations open up the opportunity for real partnership in teacher development.

Another benefit of Video Observation is that it can help those who support teacher development to more quickly differentiate their follow-up support, in dosage, methods, and content. Suzanne Arnold, who leads the alternative certification program at University of Colorado at Denver, was struck by this benefit the first year her program imple-mented video coaching. She explains:

> We were able to recognize immediately that we had a teacher really struggling with classroom management and relationships with students. He taught in a large high school, and given the school's size and how early into the school year they were, the administrators had no idea the extent to which this teacher

was challenged. Our coaches were able to get to that teacher, offer him intensive support quickly, and connect him to those within his school who could help him improve. Without video footage from baseline observations, I don't know how long he and his students may have floundered.

Likewise, we can recognize quickly those teachers who have the basics of management and instruction down and are ready to deepen their pedagogical content knowledge, for example. We can tailor their ongoing support to what is at their zone of proximal development.

How do you implement Video Observation?

There are two different types of Video Observation: Self-Reflection and Partner-Supported Reflection. Both types are described in terms of a single event; however, it is recommended that teachers regularly or semi-regularly examine videos of their own teaching. Guidance for implementing each version follows.

Self-Reflection

During **Self-Reflection**, an individual teacher engages in:

PLANNING

- **Reflect on professional development goals and incoming beliefs about the classroom.**
  Before capturing video, the teacher thinks about his or her professional development goals and current self-assessment of teaching and learning in the classroom. This planning work helps the teacher decide what instruction to capture and view. This initial reflection takes approximately 30 minutes.

EXECUTION

- **Determine what aspect of instruction to film and capture it.**

  The aspects of instructional practice captured depend on a teacher's goals. A teacher might capture a routine episode of classroom life, simply to understand the present-day instructional situation relative to aspirations. Or a teacher could record footage demonstrating a part of instruction he or she has been working to improve. The teacher could choose to capture the same 10 minutes of each class period, to look for patterns and outliers in interactions with students. Or the teacher might focus recording on a subset of students who they want to better understand. Plan for teachers to spend about five minutes determining what to capture and recording it.

- **View footage and make comments within the video platform.**

  Comments should include strengths and areas for growth, often referring to a rubric or other guidepost detailing what excellent teaching and learning entails. Recording comments promotes active engagement in Self-Reflection while preserving the teacher's analysis should they decide to invite someone to discussion. Self-Reflection often leads the teacher to generate ideas for how to better respond to student needs or otherwise refine his or her own practice. Teachers should plan to spend roughly one-and-a-half times the runtime of the chosen video clip to view and analyze it.

- **Optionally, choose to discuss reflections with a peer or a coach.**

  Depending on personal learning preferences and the availability of thought partners, the teacher may choose to invite a partner to discuss his or her reflections. Having partners to process ideas, share impressions, or playback what they heard the teacher say can be valuable, even if those partners haven't seen the lesson themselves. If teachers prefer to discuss their analysis with others, hold about 30 minutes for that work.

While Self-Reflection is a useful habit for all educators to develop, teachers who are operating at a solid level of proficiency within the classroom and who already have strong spotting and interpreting skills will likely get the most benefit from it. Teachers facing significant challenges or who find it difficult to identify and make meaning of what matters most when viewing videos might not have the skillset needed to make this independent activity as worthwhile as other strategies.

In total, Self-Reflection can happen over several days. Planning takes only about 30 minutes, as the teacher reflects on goals and current classroom realities. Execution takes between 15 minutes and one hour to complete, depending on the length of the video and whether the teacher engages in discussion with others.

Partner-Supported Reflection

In **Partner-Supported Reflection,** a teacher joins forces with someone who is supporting his or her development to observe and analyze classroom instruction and to determine what to do next to fuel improvement. This partner might be an instructional coach, an administrator, a mentor, or a colleague.

Though instructional coaches are often the partner in this version of Video Observation, it is beyond the scope of this playbook to offer a thorough treatment of effective coaching relationships or of the various models for instructional coaching in use in schools today. To learn more about instructional coaching, we suggest looking into the work of Jim Knight and Elena Aguilar as a starting point.

There are many styles of Partner-Supported Reflection, each with varying steps. Here, we offer a version that emphasizes the possibilities of a fully-virtualized learning strategy.

PLANNING

- **Align on professional development goals and incoming beliefs about the classroom.**

  Before capturing video, the teacher and reflection partner discuss the teacher's professional development goals and his or her incoming beliefs about the state of the classroom. This planning work is important because it influences what instruction the teacher decides to capture and share with the partner. For instance, if a teacher describes feeling overwhelmed and unsure of what's going well or causing challenge in the classroom, the partner may advise capturing longer lengths of classroom footage to examine. This initial conversation takes approximately 30 minutes.

EXECUTION

- **Teacher captures and shares one or more video clips to watch.**

  The purpose of viewing and analyzing these clips is to identify instructional strengths to extend and areas to improve, in relation to the teacher's professional development goals. In this version of the learning strategy, either teacher or partner can select sections of video footage for analysis, depending on the nature of the partnership and the developmental needs of the teacher.

  As in Self-Reflection, the specific segments of videos chosen depend on the teacher's goals. If a teacher is selecting segments of video to analyze, he or she can plan to spend about 5 minutes determining what to view. If a partner is selecting clips, he or she is most likely less familiar with the footage captured and may need up to 20 minutes choosing the right portions for analysis.

- **Both teacher and partner view selected footage and make comments within the video platform.**

  More developed, self-reflective teachers might self-analyze first and then invite the partner to react. Less self-reflective teachers might ask their partner to offer comments first. Plan to spend roughly one-and-a-half times the total runtime of the chosen clips to view and analyze.

- **Discuss reflections on video analysis.**

  The teacher and partner can begin discussion by reviewing and replying to one another's comments, in order to align on those areas of strength to extend and points of weakness to improve. Depending on teacher preference and the degree of alignment in their analysis, the teacher and partner may choose to continue discussion via video conference.

  Though both people should have input, any specific changes a teacher decides to make in his or her classroom should be owned by the teacher instead of prescribed by the partner. Without this ownership, the teacher is not likely to commit to the next steps needed to make change. Hold about 30 minutes for this work.

- **Jointly determine next steps to support development.**

  Based on the analysis and discussion of the evidence, the pair determines next steps to support teacher development. These next steps can include participating in more cycles of Partner-Supported Reflection or engaging in additional professional learning strategies, including those outlined in this playbook.

  To extend an area of instructional strength, consider pairing a teacher with peers to whom the teacher might offer support, asking the teacher's permission to share his or her video footage in future professional development, or supporting the teacher to deepen that area of strength even further.

  The teacher and his or her partner should budget between 20-40 minutes for this next-steps conversation.

In total, Partner-Supported Reflection can happen over approximately one week. In the planning phase, the teacher and partner spend approximately 30 minutes. The teacher and partner should each budget 75-90 minutes for the execution phase, depending on the length of the video.

SKILL BUILDING SEQUENCE

Debbie Armendariz serves as Portland Public Schools' Director of Elementary Programs. She wants to ensure that bilingual teachers in the dual-language department's licensure program are developing concrete teaching skills. Debbie's team of coaches has envisioned professional development that asks teachers to spiral through three instructional practices with increasing complexity and competency throughout the year.

Teachers start the year examining the skill of communicating learning objectives. Coaches introduce the targeted skill and have teachers analyze an example video. Teachers then try to implement the skill, capturing footage of themselves communicating objectives to students in their own classrooms. Afterward, the teachers analyze that footage in collaboration with a coach to determine where they are in their skill development. Coaches and teachers engage in discussion via threaded comments within the video and in one-on-one conversation.

After the first sequence, they examine the instructional practice of gradually releasing responsibility and then of structuring student interactions. Later in the year, teachers return to the initial skill of communicating objectives. This second sequence is focused on implementing the skill with increased complexity, by confirming student understanding of the objective, explaining how the objective will be assessed, and supporting students in assessing themselves against the objective.

In this way, Debbie's team is able to get a quick and accurate assessment of teachers' skill development and deepen their instructional practice over time.

What is a Skill Building Sequence?

In **Skill Building Sequence,** teachers watch and analyze an example video that models a specific skill, enact that specific skill in a video of their own, and share footage with a coach, in order to provide a checkpoint for their skill development.

Skill Building Sequence combines Example Analysis with Video Observations and is structured and guided by a teacher educator or instructional coach. The sequence begins when the coach chooses a video that models a teaching skill that is in focus for the individual or group of teachers. For example, clips might illustrate a particular instructional practice, like leading a whole-class discussion, or show a lesson or activity for a specific content-area, like read aloud in an elementary literacy classroom.

After Example Analysis, teachers enact that same skill in their own classrooms. It is important that teachers implement the skill with their students and not just a role play or rehearsal. Although there can be value in teachers trying to mimic a practice they've seen modeled, they need opportunities to enact it in a real classroom setting to strengthen their judgment about how to flexibly employ it for the benefit of their specific students.

Teachers capture footage of themselves implementing the skill and then share clips for input from a coach or teacher educator and sometimes from a peer. Teachers watch their own footage, comparing it to the example that launched the sequence, and discuss their observations with others. Coaches and teachers use this learning strategy as a way to check on how the teacher is implementing a new skill. The analysis of teachers' strengths and areas for refinement helps both coach and teacher structure follow-up support.

What are the benefits and impact of Skill Building Sequence?

Skill Building Sequence offers several benefits to teachers and coaches. By engaging in structured rounds of skill building, teachers can systematically strengthen and deepen their skills and judgment, while also developing self-reflective habits. For some teachers, simply having a specific skill to work on and comparing their own implementation to an example helps jump-start their improvement, even before a coach or peer supports them. In this way, Skill Building Sequence offers the opportunity for teachers to take control, even within a coach-directed professional learning strategy. As instructional coach David Baker shares:

> In a Skill Building Sequence focused on questioning, a teacher reached out to me and shared that she had viewed the footage she uploaded, compared it to the example video that had begun the sequence, and wasn't satisfied. She wanted to try the skill again with her students before sharing for input from me and her peers. My reaction was "By all means! You watched evidence of your practice, you weren't happy, and you want to work on it before you even share? Go right ahead!" That teacher took four to five more takes, working to improve it at each turn, before she shared with others. The depth of her practice had accelerated because she was in control of the learning. She was in control of what she recorded and who else saw it. She used evidence of her practice to improve.

Skill Building Sequence allows instructional coaches to personalize and target their work with teachers. Coaches can see concrete evidence of what teachers are able to implement, and then alter their follow-up support in response. Suzanne Arnold, a teacher educator, shared that before they used Skill Building Sequence, "I rarely got the opportunity to even see people working on what we were teaching them to do in coursework. This activity allows us to be much more focused in our support of teachers."

How do you implement Skill Building Sequence?

PLANNING

- **Choose an example video clip and share it online.**

  This clip should feature the skill or practice selected for being part of a predefined teacher learning sequence or for representing the next area of development in the teacher's individual learning trajectory. Reference the Example Analysis chapter for more guidance on choosing example clips. Those selecting example video clips and structuring teachers' analysis should plan to spend about 30 minutes on this step.

- **Facilitate teachers' analysis of the example.**

  In this learning strategy, it's preferable to structure teachers' analysis instead of leaving it unguided—to ensure teachers can break down, spot, and interpret the most important aspects of the skill they're striving to incorporate into their own instruction. Guide teachers to spot the technical moves demonstrated in the example, but also to weigh the considerations the example teacher made when determining how to enact a skill with a particular set of students working in specific content ideas. Help teachers analyze the effect of the teacher skill on students' thinking. Scaffolding will help support these types of analyses. Those people structuring teachers' analysis of example videos should plan to spend about 20 minutes assembling guidance, linking to observational frameworks or rubrics, and developing guiding questions.

EXECUTION

- **Teachers view and analyze the skill or instructional practice featured in the example video.**

  Using guidance provided, teachers should spend roughly double the total run time of the example video to complete their analysis, annotating that video with comments to facilitate their examination.

- **Teachers enact the featured skill with students, capture video, and share it with others.**

  Teachers should select footage which reflects the implementation of the targeted skill and share it with a coach and potentially with peers who are engaged in the same learning sequence. In most cases, 5-15 minutes of video is sufficient to capture implementation of the key skill.

- **Teachers and others analyze and discuss their footage.**

  Reference specific guidance in the Video Observations chapter as you prepare to implement this step. In Skill Building Sequence, more self-reflective and skilled teachers might use Self-Reflection while other teachers might use Partner-Supported Reflection. Teachers and all observers should spend roughly double the total run time of the video to complete and discuss their analysis.

In total, Skill Building Sequence can happen over one to several weeks. Budget about 50 minutes for planning this learning strategy. Execution takes 25-75 minutes for teachers and 10-30 minutes for partners who are analyzing teacher footage, depending on the length of video clips.

VIDEO LEARNING COMMUNITY

Rebekah Stathakis is an adjunct lecturer at Northwestern University, where she supports Humanities teachers through their practicum and student teaching experiences. Rebekah believes that teachers improve their practice when they work collaboratively to analyze concrete evidence of student thinking and learning. To encourage her middle and high school teacher candidates to build this habit, Rebekah places them in groups that meet across two quarters of the academic year to view and analyze classroom footage.

Rebekah establishes areas of focus for most of the videos teachers record. For instance, early in the first quarter, teachers capture and analyze three-to-five minutes of footage featuring evidence of student thinking, whether a small group discussion of the causes of the Civil War, a partner conversation in French about plans for an upcoming weekend, or one student's response to a question about a particular line in a novel. Teachers view the footage together, aiming to identify what students know, what misconceptions they may have, and what instructional steps would support that student to move forward, and make comments within the video about specific moments that lead them to conclusions about students.

As the facilitator of synchronous and asynchronous discussions, Rebekah tries to be involved in her teacher's substantive conversations as little as possible. She challenges teachers to justify the conclusions they are drawing with evidence from their students, but beyond that, she strives to do very little of the analysis herself. In this way, she supports teachers to build their interpretive skills and to develop confidence that they can improve their practice if they focus on understanding and responding to students.

As the quarter progresses, Rebekah's students capture, share, analyze and discuss brief episodes of teaching and learning on a variety of topics, including guiding class discussions, offering feedback, supporting students to carry the cognitive load, and other topics that are identified as areas of needs for teachers themselves, such as how to engage students who tend to stay quiet in the classroom. Rebekah finds that as teachers in video groups build trust with one another, they begin to call on one another to look at other moments of instruction, outside of those Rebekah has identified. Teachers also begin to reference what they have learned from their peers' clips, noting when they are trying a strategy they observed in someone else's video or when they are acting upon a conclusion the group came to in discussion.

What is Video Learning Community?

In **Video Learning Community** teachers view, analyze, and discuss footage of one another's classrooms in order to fuel collective improvement of the community members. Video Learning Communities (VLCs) draw inspiration from Professional Learning Communities (PLCs), popularized by the work of Richard DuFour, who pioneered the construct. To learn more about Professional Learning Communities, we recommend starting with *Learning by Doing: A Handbook for Professional Learning Communities at Work*, by Richard DuFour et al. (2006).

Similar to PLCs, VLCs are collaborative, ongoing groups that work to maximize teacher and student learning. Unlike PLCs, VLCs operate in a virtual environment, placing classroom video footage at the center of the community's work. Members of VLCs capture classroom footage to share with colleagues, so their peers can collaboratively discuss the state of student learning and the ways instruction influences it. While this learning strategy includes component steps from Video Observations, VLCs use those steps for the goal of collective learning instead of individual teacher improvement.

Teachers choose video footage to share, keeping in mind some question that the entire community would benefit from examining. They might choose clips to help the community spot and interpret the extent or depth of student learning and the factors contributing to that reality. Alternatively, teachers might share footage of an area of teaching and learning the group has already identified as key to improving student results. For example, teachers could share video of their efforts to help students use the precise academic language of a discipline more consistently. VLC members analyze and compare shared footage, identifying evidence of what students are able to do, and then offer feedback or identify best practice and helpful resources.

Rebekah Stathakis finds that relatively short episodes of classroom footage, usually five minutes or less, are best for shared analysis. In her experience, teachers become overwhelmed by all there is to spot and discuss within a 15-20 minute clip. Instead, she prompts teachers to find the 3-5 minute segment of footage that is most interesting, rich, or important, and engage in deep analysis of that segment. This narrow focus helps teachers closely examine all the evidence of student thinking, learning, and well-being present in the footage.

VLCs are most often directed by teachers, who make comments within video clips about their interpretation of students and of teaching. However, the community can also be supported by a facilitator. Members of the VLC can choose to implement discussion protocols or can have organic conversation about their analysis. Because VLCs operate for more than one cycle, the community builds shared knowledge over time, continuously improving teaching and learning.

What are the benefits and impact of Video Learning Community?

Video Learning Community offers many benefits. VLCs can support individual teachers to drive their own professional learning by deeply analyzing evidence of student thinking in videos and by using peer analysis and feedback as a source of help. Discussions within VLCs can strengthen teachers' skills at spotting and interpreting areas for change in classrooms and at comparing multiple pieces of evidence.

Video Learning Communities have been shown to strengthen teaching in classrooms by building teachers' abilities to see, understand, and respond to students. Miriam Sherin of Northwestern University and Beth van Es of University of California-Irvine have studied a model for VLCs that they developed and term "video clubs." These scholars found that after a year of participation in a video club, middle school math teachers were better able to pay attention to and reason about student ideas, both when analyzing video and during live classroom instruction (Sherin and van Es, 2009). Additionally, they observed that participating elementary teachers were better able to elicit and probe student thinking and more frequently position themselves as mathematical learners in the classroom by working through the math with students or considering ideas raised by students (van Es and Sherin, 2010).

Beyond the possible benefits for individual teachers, VLCs can encourage members to take responsibility for the learning of all students and for the instructional practices enacted across classrooms. In a profession characterized by individual improvement behind one's own classroom door, VLCs can help teachers improve collectively. And these collective efforts mean that VLCs have the potential to help entire schools operate as learning organizations, able to continuously grow and adapt as a result of reflecting on the experience and results of its children and teachers.

How do you implement Video Learning Community?

PLANNING

- **Initiate VLCs and support their launch as a learning strategy.**
  Support the launch of a VLC by sharing aspirations for what it can accomplish for the school community and by guiding teachers to appoint a facilitator and to establish a regular schedule. Plan to spend about 30 minutes planning the parameters for VLCs and another 30-60 minutes communicating those ideas with teachers. Teachers will need to spend only 10 minutes reading or talking about the guidance.

EXECUTION

- **VLC members establish a specific purpose for viewing video clips and a schedule for analyzing and discussing footage.**
  The VLC can determine a purpose for viewing video clips based on the group's current level of clarity on the state of learning for all students and what is contributing and hindering their progress. If the group already has that clarity, VLC members can determine a relevant area of instruction for analysis. If the group does not yet have that clarity, then initial videos might feature routine instruction, so that members can spot interactions of significance and work to interpret their effect on students. In this step, a facilitator can play an important role in steering the group toward consensus.

  VLCs might choose to have all members record and share classroom footage aligned to the established purpose every time video is shared. Alternatively, VLCs might establish a rotating schedule, so that teachers take turns sharing footage over the course of a school year. Participating teachers should view footage from all VLC members' classrooms at least once.

  VLC members should plan to spend between 30-60 minutes to establish purposes and schedules for their work.

- **Members record and share footage aligned to the established purpose.**
  Consider advising each teacher to conduct a self-analysis first, by leaving comments that guide his or her colleagues as they review the shared clips. Teachers should budget an amount of time at least equal to the total run time of the video if engaging in self-analysis.

- **Members view and analyze shared clips.**
  VLC members use relevant focusing techniques from chapter 3 of this playbook to support their analysis of shared clips. Teachers should budget double the total runtime of the videos under review for this work.

- **Members discuss video.**
  If VLCs use purely synchronous conversation, the facilitator might review uploaded video in advance and select a clip that he or she believes will promote rich and relevant learning. In the conversation, VLC members can ask the facilitator to pause the video at certain moments to share comments and ask questions of one another.

  If VLCs use a blended format, participants might begin discussion by reviewing and responding to one another's comments. Then, the facilitator can review the video and related online commentary and identify a few exchanges ripe for synchronous discussion. Reviewing the online commentary in advance allows for a more targeted real-time discussion with organic back-and-forth dialogue between VLC members.

  Discussions of video evidence can range from roughly double video runtime for asynchronous discussions, to one to two hours for a blended format.

- **Members determine whether to maintain or adjust the purpose for the next round of video analysis.**

  A VLC might engage in only one or in several cycles of video work related to an established purpose before determining that its members have made sufficient progress or have gleaned enough insight. At that point, the VLC can establish a different purpose and begin sharing and analyzing related videos anew. This decision-making can happen at the conclusion of discussion of videos.

- **Outside of formal VLC meetings, members can prompt one another to view and analyze footage.**

  As teachers grow comfortable with one another and begin to experience the value of having peers analyze their video footage, they can prompt one another to examine footage of their practice beyond the videos selected for formal meetings of the Video Learning Community.

In total, Video Learning Community can operate over a period of months or an entire school year. In the planning phase, facilitators should spend 60-90 minutes and participating teachers should plan to spend 10 minutes. For each round of video analysis, participating teachers should plan to spend between two and three-and-a-half hours.

STRATEGY 8

VIRTUAL WALK-THROUGH

Maria Martinez is the department head of a ten-person mathematics team in a large high school. Seeking to keep a pulse on trends in teaching and learning in a way that is feasible given the size of the department and her own classroom teaching responsibilities, Maria commits to popping into every classroom for about five minutes at three different points during the year. To facilitate this, Maria asks every teacher in her department to share footage of one full lesson in a two-week period in October, January, and April. She then selects a brief segment of each teacher's lesson to view.

In a meeting in September, Maria works with the teachers on her team to establish what she will look for in October pop-in observations. Teachers are eager for Maria to look for evidence of students making sense of problems and persevering in solving them and to highlight aspects of their instruction that are helping or hindering students.

In the first two weeks of October, teachers capture and share with Maria a sample lesson. The following week, Maria views a five-minute segment of every teacher's video. In total, Maria spends about 15 minutes per teacher viewing, analyzing, and leaving specific feedback, based on the "look-fors" established by her department.

At the end of the month, Maria reflects on her analysis across classrooms. By reading back over her annotated comments, she surfaces trends across students and teachers and makes notes of any outlier classrooms that may need additional support or accelerated opportunities for growth. Maria leaves this reflection time with significant clarity about how the academic year has gotten started in the math department and how she needs to focus upcoming team meetings.

What is Virtual Walk-Through?

In **Virtual Walk-Through,** observers view short segments of lesson-length video footage, aiming to identify trends in teaching and learning across classrooms and to provide accurate and specific feedback to teachers. This strategy is analogous to the style of observations conducted by administrators as they walk through the school building, popping into classrooms to observe instruction for about five minutes. To learn more about this style of walk-through observations, see *Classroom Walkthroughs to Improve Teaching and Learning,* by Donald Kachur et al. (2010), and *The Three-Minute Classroom Walk-Through*, by Carolyn J. Downey et al. (2004).

In a virtual setting, instead of popping into rooms, observers access teachers' uploaded lesson-length footage and view short segments from them. Instead of leaving a sticky note with feedback, observers annotate the segment of footage viewed or have a virtual or live discussion with the teacher. While coaches and administrators are often observers, Virtual Walk-Through affords people new to observation or with responsibilities that preclude them from observing during the regular school day the opportunity to participate.

What are the benefits and impact of Virtual Walk-Through?

Virtual Walk-Through can help the observer understand the general state of teaching and learning in the school and how it is evolving over time. It can also help teachers receive support from an instructional leader.

A summary of available research on the impact of classroom walk-throughs by Jane David (2008) shows that administrators find the practice useful in discerning the degree to which teachers are successfully implementing agreed-upon practices and in adjusting professional development in response. Other studies have found that walk-throughs help create a shared vision for high-quality instruction, particularly when observers use a common rubric.

In addition to those benefits, David also describes risks of this learning strategy. She notes that for those being observed, walk-throughs can be perceived as evaluative and unhelpful. To mitigate that risk, take care to build a trusting culture, establish a clear purpose for walk-throughs, and share relevant and actionable feedback in a timely manner.

How do you implement Virtual Walk-Through?

PLANNING

- **Determine who will observe.**
  Because Virtual Walk-Through requires less effort to plan and implement, people with sound instructional judgment but limited time have a way to add value to teaching and learning across their school. What matters most is that observers have a strong understanding of high-quality instruction and can conduct online walk-through observations with some regularity. Plan to spend about 15 minutes determining who will be an observer for this version of the strategy.

- **Establish the purpose of walk-through observations with teachers.**
  Walk-through observations are not evaluative. To help build this nonevaluative mind-set, establish look-fors and listen-fors to ground walk-through observations. These look- and listen-fors can focus on many aspects of instruction, from student engagement, to explanations and representations of core content, to pedagogical strategies, to implementation of curriculum, to differentiating to meet individual student's

needs. Plan to spend about an hour working with teachers to establish the purpose.

- **Set a schedule for teachers to upload entire lessons and for observers to hold time to review brief segments of those videos.**
  To mimic the effect of popping into classrooms, ask teachers to upload footage of an entire lesson on whatever schedule you establish. If the goal is to virtually walk-through every classroom once a week, then teachers should upload one full lesson a week. Similarly, observers should schedule and protect time to observe. As a guideline, building-level administrators or instructional coaches may consider a schedule that allows for observing every classroom at least once a month. Plan to spend about 15 minutes establishing the schedule for teachers to share videos and for observers to review them. Guide teachers to spend 10 minutes planning their uploading schedule for the year.

EXECUTION

- **On the established schedule, selected teachers record and share entire lessons.**
  Teachers share video footage of full lessons on whatever schedule was established initially. Because teachers do not need to determine what portions of the lesson to share, this step should take no more than five minutes to complete.

- **Observers view and analyze consistent short chunks of multiple teachers' lessons and follow-up to support teachers' growth.**
  Observers should choose to watch the same short segment from each lesson they view, like the first five minutes or an eight-minute section in the middle. Analysis should focus on the established look-fors and listen-fors.

  For this learning strategy to benefit teachers, observers must follow-up in a timely manner. This can involve sharing targeted feedback and probing questions through online comments, engaging in discussion, asking observed teachers to share what support they need, or recommending specific resources (e.g., classrooms to observe, articles to read, etc.) and learning activities.

The amount of time needed to view and analyze footage and to follow-up with teachers will depend on how many classrooms are observed per week. For each classroom observed, hold at least 10 minutes to view and analyze footage and to follow-up with teachers. Aim to offer that follow-up in the week following the virtual pop-in.

- **Observers reflect on trends and outliers across classrooms and identify implications.**
  After a full round of Virtual Walk-Through, observers pause to take stock of and note overarching patterns across classrooms. This can be done by skimming back over feedback shared with teachers, reviewing discussion notes, and discussing with other observers. Identify the implications of these patterns for professional development, curriculum decisions, relational work, school climate efforts, and more. Plan to spend 30-60 minutes for this reflection.

In total, an entire school building can engage in Virtual Walk-Through in about a month, depending on the numbers of classrooms and observers. Initial planning takes about 90 minutes for the planner and 10 minutes for teachers. Regular walk-throughs will take each observer at least 10 minutes per teacher per cycle and will take each teacher no more than five minutes. Reflection at the end of a round of Virtual Walk-Through should take observers 30-60 minutes.

STRATEGY 9

VIDEO ROUNDS

For the last few months, assistant principal James Jackson has been supporting his high school English Language Arts teachers to engage students in close reading of grade-level texts. Though James has structured professional development time to allow teachers to analyze example videos of close reading instruction and to plan upcoming lessons together, neither principal nor teachers have stepped back to see the effects of that PD on teaching and learning across classrooms.

To create that opportunity, James asks all eight ELA teachers to capture and share 10-minute segments of their close reading instruction. To focus the analysis of these clips, James offers the following prompt: "Are students able to make a claim about the text, support it with evidence, and explain their reasoning clearly? Is there a difference in their ability to do so in writing versus in conversation, or with fiction versus nonfiction text? In what ways are teachers supporting students to do this textual analysis?"

Each teacher analyzes and comments on his or her own footage and at least two of their peers' clips, while James watches at least five minutes of footage from every classroom filmed and reviews the comments teachers have left for one another. In the next department meeting, the assistant principal and teachers focus their discussion on a pattern they observed across classrooms. Consistently, students were challenged to make and support claims about texts for which they had little background knowledge. They decide that teachers should develop and implement brief instructional activities that will expose all students to the relevant prerequisite knowledge upon which a specific text is built, before students engage in close reading. Teachers agree to try this in the next reading unit and to upload and examine new footage in six weeks.

What are Video Rounds?

Video Rounds is a facilitator-driven learning strategy that focuses on school or system-wide improvement. In this learning strategy, members of a Video Rounds team analyze and discuss footage from a broad set of classrooms to fuel a process of inquiry and problem-solving, determine the impact of prior professional development, or align around a common vision for excellent teaching and learning.

Video Rounds has similarities to instructional rounds pioneered by Elizabeth City et al. (2009) at Harvard Graduate School of Education and teacher rounds developed by Thomas Del Prete (1997) at Clark University. These rounds were modeled after medical rounds, a primary source of field-based professional learning for doctors. In instructional rounds, groups of educators within a school, larger system, or broader ecosystem work together to improve instruction by establishing a goal for their shared work, observing multiple classrooms to gather evidence related to that goal, and collaborating to develop strategies that will lead to improvements beyond a single classroom (City, 2011). To learn more about instructional rounds, we recommend starting with *Instructional rounds in education: A network approach to improving teaching and learning* by Elizabeth City et al. (2009).

Video Rounds move this work to a virtual environment. Rather than observing live within classrooms, participants view classroom footage aligned with the purpose of the round. For instance, if the focus of a round is on supporting students' reasoning, teachers across disciplinary areas could be asked to capture videos of the ways in which students make claims, provide evidence to support those claims, and justify the relevance of that evidence. Then, when it suits individuals within some preestablished span of time, all participants on a Video Rounds team can view and compare the same set of videos to prepare for discussion with others on the team.

The discussion in Video Rounds centers around using evidence from across the observed classrooms to agree upon trends and outliers. After establishing trends, participants work to define what will be true in terms of student learning should the trends continue (City, 2011). Then, interpreting the collective evidence, the team works to determine the contextual factors that might contribute to the trends. From there, the Video Rounds team determines how to focus future professional learning opportunities to support teachers and build needed capacity across the system.

Video Rounds and Virtual Walk-Through have much in common. Both learning strategies are highly collaborative and involve identifying trends across classrooms. However, Video Rounds is distinguished from Video Walk-Through because it is geared toward supporting collective inquiry into a school-wide challenge as opposed to offering specific, accurate, and actionable feedback to classroom teachers.

What are the benefits and impact of Video Rounds?

Video Rounds support a collective approach to improving teaching and learning across an entire school or system. Rounds can help educators across a variety of functional roles align around a clear, shared, and specific definition of excellent instruction because everyone has reviewed and discussed the same evidence in-depth. They can empower classroom teachers to take responsibility for school- or system-wide improvements by asking them to work side-by-side with administrators to find solutions to shared challenges and by allowing them to ask directly for the support they need in order to improve. This collective approach to improvement can combat the mythology of the "solo genius" instructional leader—a leader who supposedly holds all the answers to problems in the school (Aguilar, 2014). Video

Rounds can also enable culture-building and development of Video Learning Communities.

These rounds can also provide a helpful mirror to those who design professional learning opportunities for teachers. By seeing what is happening across classrooms, it's possible to assess the degree to which teachers are consistently able to act on what they've learned in workshops, coaching, or curricular initiatives. Video evidence collected can also be reused for Example Analysis and other future professional learning activities.

Video Rounds also offers the benefit of reducing the logistical complexity of in-person instructional rounds, which can be burdensome at best and prohibitive at worst. In-person rounds involve multiple people trying to visit multiple classrooms at the same time. Often, this logistical hurdle makes instructional rounds more possible for administrators than for teachers themselves. The realities of classroom interruptions, schedule changes, and the like can also mean that observers may see instruction that is misaligned to the larger goal of the round.

Instead of spending significant time coordinating in-person classroom visits and arranging coverage for teachers who are observers, Video Rounds planners simply need to establish a schedule for uploading and viewing footage. As long as the guidance provided to classroom teachers is clear, Video Rounds team members can be reasonably certain that the instruction they view will be aligned to the purpose of the round. Spending less time on planning logistics allows the school to maximize time and focus on implementing the learning strategy itself.

How do you implement Video Rounds?

PLANNING

- **Establish a purpose and a Video Rounds team.**
  Begin by establishing a purpose at an administrative or leadership team level. Alternately, assemble the Video Rounds team

first, then involve its members in determining the purpose for rounds. Both approaches offer benefits.

Because Video Rounds are a tool for structured inquiry, it can be useful to frame the purpose as a question. For example, "Are students engaged in the academic work of the class? Are there differences in the level of engagement between subgroups of students? How would we characterize the type of student engagement we see—is it compliance-based or does it indicate deeper student ownership of the work?"

There are no hard rules about who should be on the Video Rounds team. They can include both administrators and classroom teachers, either from within one content area or grade-level or from a broader set of classrooms. They can also include university faculty and student teachers, if rounds are happening within a broader educational ecosystem.

Budget two to three hours to establish a purpose and assemble the Video Rounds team.

- **Build a schedule.**
Develop a schedule for when teachers should share relevant video evidence, when Video Rounds team members will analyze videos, and when team discussions will occur. Ask team members to view uploaded clips within a common timeframe (e.g., within one week). Depending on the number of videos relative to people on the team, consider whether to ask everyone to review the same evidence or to jigsaw video clips across the team so that at least two people have viewed every clip. Plan to spend 30 minutes on this step.

- **Select a representative set of teachers to share video evidence.**
Once you've established a purpose for the rounds, ask a representative set of classroom teachers to upload relevant video

evidence to the online platform. This set can include both teachers who are and aren't part of the Video Rounds team. Select at least five classrooms to observe, to begin developing a sense of patterns. Budget about an hour to share the request with teachers and have any necessary conversation to ensure their agreement and comfort.

- **Provide teachers clear guidance on what to capture.**
  Give teachers tasked with recording their classrooms clear parameters about what to capture, so that the team ends up having parallel video evidence across classrooms. For example, if the team has decided to focus on student engagement, ask teachers to collect and upload footage from the beginning of a lesson, in the same period of the same day. However, if the team is working on something more specific, like students' academic discourse, ask teachers to determine a lesson within a given few days that presents opportunities for discussion and upload the footage they capture. Those planning Video Rounds should plan to spend about 20 minutes on this step.

EXECUTION

- **Representative teachers capture relevant video footage.**
  Using shared guidance, teachers uploading footage should spend less than 10 minutes preparing and sharing clips.

- **Video Rounds team members analyze relevant video evidence.**
  Prompt team members to use the Spot and Compare focusing techniques to identify and comment on moments within individual videos and patterns across videos that seem important relative to the established purpose. If the team is striving to build alignment around a shared framework for teaching and learning, prompt them to Break Down instruction into its component parts, using language from those frameworks. All

of this analysis can happen individually, from the comfort of team members' own work-spaces as their schedules permit. Alternately, if convenient and desired, team members can get together online or in-person to review videos with others on the team. To analyze footage, team members should plan to spend double the total run time of the videos.

- **Prepare for and engage the team in discussion to identify action steps.**
  To prepare for facilitation, review comments team members have made within uploaded videos to identify areas of widespread agreement and areas of divergent perspective. Consider using a discussion protocol with guiding questions that help the team maintain a nonjudgmental stance and ground their decision-making in fueling student learning.

  The meeting planner should plan to spend an hour reviewing commentary within videos and preparing for the team conversation. Budget 60-90 minutes for the meeting itself. The facilitator or note-taker should hold an additional hour to record and share finalized action steps.

- **Complete action steps identified in the discussion.**
  Depending on the team's specific understanding of trends and conclusions about underlying causes, a variety of people might leave the meeting with action items intended to help the school make progress. Action items might include planning specific professional development, gathering resources to support teachers, or addressing operational issues, for example. Those who leave with specific action items should reserve a handful of hours for their work.

- **Repeat video analysis and discussion, as needed.**
  Keep the team engaged in Video Rounds by continuing cycles of analysis and discussion until the team sees evidence that the

school has made sufficient progress toward the purpose of the rounds. At such time, the team can either disband or determine a new purpose for the next cycle of Video Rounds.

In total, Video Rounds can happen over several weeks or months. The work in the planning stage of Video Rounds will take the planner four-to-five hours. To implement one cycle of Video Rounds, the planner spends five to eight hours and team members spend approximately five hours, depending on the number and type of action steps identified.

S T R A T E G Y   1 0

LONGER-RANGE REFLECTION

Megan Kelley-Petersen directs the alternative certification program in the College of Education at the University of Washington. She wants to encourage teachers in her program to recognize their growth over time, particularly because these teachers, learning so much on the job day-to-day, often don't recognize that they are improving.

Toward the end of the school year, Megan asks teachers to watch the very first video they shared online, followed by one of their most recently captured clips. She offers several prompts to help them consider the ways they have grown and what has enabled their learning. Teachers put together a brief presentation to share with their teacher educator and peers in their certification cohort. Some teachers choose a 30-second clip from a video, while others share a piece of student work, or a screenshot of a specific student. This video or image serves as a springboard for a story about their growth as a first-year teacher.

A common theme in teacher presentations is the way in which they've gotten better at seeing and hearing children. Many note how their first video showed them focused on getting students to be still and compliant while the teacher talked. In contrast, their end-of-year clips show them working to elicit and respond to students' ideas and to connect students to one another. While teachers may have been aware of this shift in their practice, watching the beginning- and end-of-year clips together creates a powerful, visceral reflection experience. Megan believes this end-of-year reflection ritual helps teachers solidify how much they have grown and what further growth is possible when they regularly reflect on video evidence.

What is Longer-Range Reflection?

Longer-Range Reflection involves teachers reviewing and comparing video footage of their instruction and related commentary over some period of time, in order to identify what they have learned, how they have grown, and what has contributed to that development. The exact period of time teachers look back can vary—from a marking period, to a semester, to a full school year. Teachers can compare footage from the beginning and end of that timeframe, or they can compare multiple points across the range.

Having an online archive of all past clips and related commentary allows teachers a rich library of evidence to choose from and examine. That evidence serves as the benchmark against which they can measure to determine progress and identify lessons learned.

Teachers can analyze videos to spot the broad ways they have grown. Or, they might look at a narrower set of specific skills that they prioritized developing and see how they've improved. In addition to seeing changes in their performance on video, teachers can examine related commentary and use the interpret focusing technique to trace the evolution of their underlying assumptions and beliefs about students, teaching and learning, or the role of a teacher. This critical analysis can help teachers consider the effect of those underlying beliefs on their actions in the classroom.

What are the benefits and impact of Longer-Range Reflection?

The primary benefit of Longer-Range Reflection is that it enables evidence-based reflection of progress over time. When teachers are asked to reflect on how they've developed and what they've learned, they have the opportunity to build what Carol Dweck (2006) terms a "growth mind-set," or the belief that with dedication and effort, they can improve as professionals.

Teachers at all stages of their careers can benefit from this learning strategy. Brand-new or early career teachers, in particular, may operate in survival mode. As Nancy Jaeger, director of a teacher residency, explains, "A year of residency and working on licensure is daunting. In Longer-Range Reflection, teachers can see evidence of the very beginner moves they made and contrast that with what they're now able to do. It is powerful for them to realize for themselves how they've grown." Nancy doesn't think teachers can outgrow the usefulness of this learning strategy and encourages her teachers to continue to use it, even after they've left the residency and no longer have a formal requirement to do so.

Longer-Range Reflection through a portfolio of evidence is a key component of many graduate degree programs and advanced certification processes like the one offered by National Board for Professional Teaching Standards. Jana Hunzicker (2011) found that teachers who have undertaken this certification process describe the reflective and analytical work they did to assemble portfolios as having a high-impact on their development as professionals.

How do you implement Longer-Range Reflection?

PLANNING

- **Determine a period of time you want teachers to consider in their reflection.**

  This strategy is a natural culminating activity to the end of a semester or school-year, though you might consider using it in even shorter cycles. Plan to spend 15 minutes or less making this decision, after considering the calendar and identifying any moments that can serve as natural reflection points.

- **Offer guidance to structure Longer-Range Reflection.**

  Depending on their strength and experience level, offer teachers whatever support they might need to think carefully about and analyze video evidence. Help teachers look for changes both in behavior and in thinking and to identify what they have learned over time. Encourage teachers to celebrate the growth they have made. Prompt them to consider areas for future growth based on what they observe in a range of clips over time. Plan to spend less than an hour structuring how you'd like teachers to reflect on the various pieces of evidence.

EXECUTION

- **Teachers view and analyze evidence from the beginning and end or from across the time period.**

  Teachers re-watch video footage and read over discussions and comments attached to those clips. Budget at least one-and-a-half times the total run time of the videos for review.

- **Consider engaging teachers in discussion of their reflection.**

  Whether in an online or in-person format, many teachers benefit from discussing their reflections with others. Group discussion can support a teacher's meaning-making and strengthen the degree to which a cohort, team, or school faculty takes responsibility for collective improvement as a professional learning community. If teachers are going to discuss Longer-Range Reflection with others, ask them to document their analysis in writing or in a recorded video reflection. Time spent discussing reflections can vary but need not take more than an hour to be valuable.

In total, Longer-Range Reflection can happen over several days. The person planning the learning strategy will need to spend about an hour determining a time period for reflection and providing teacher guidance. In execution, teachers will spend between one hour and

45 minutes to three hours to complete. If the person planning the learning strategy participates in discussion with teachers, budget an additional hour for that work.

STRATEGY 11

ITERATIVE INVESTIGATION

Over summer break, twelve teachers at Long Branch Middle School join principal Evelyn Cruz to learn about a voluntary professional development opportunity. The opportunity is to participate in self-driven cycles of inquiry and improvement, to select a partner to support them, and to leverage an online video platform. Though Evelyn puts no pressure on them to sign-up, she is pleasantly surprised when all twelve teachers do so. These twelve people vary in levels of teaching experience and self-reflectiveness.

Teachers begin the work by choosing a partner from a pool of colleagues, administrators, and a local university professor and then sharing with the partner a baseline video of instruction. Teachers analyze that video to select an area for improvement and discuss their decision-making with their partner. Some teachers decide to focus on deepening their students' critical thinking, some focus on incorporating reading and writing into science instruction, and still others elect to work on increasing students' time on task. Many teachers request specific help from their partner to craft a goal that will clarify the specific improvement they are striving to make.

With their area of improvement identified and goals set, teachers and their partners find resources to support their learning, including videos to view and research to read. Though each teacher sets his or her own pace, they all upload and examine a new classroom video to check progress at least once a quarter. Some teachers find the process so beneficial that they examine evidence more frequently.

As the year progresses, some teachers stay focused on the initial area they identified, steadily working to refine their instruction and meet their goal. Others meet the goals they set and move on to a different area of challenge.

What is Iterative Investigation?

In **Iterative Investigation**, teachers use a structured cycle of inquiry to improve teaching and learning. Teachers select an area of focus for their investigation by analyzing evidence from their classrooms and identifying a challenge that, if addressed, would meaningfully improve student outcomes. Once they have identified the challenge, teachers record baseline evidence of teaching and learning and find resources to support their learning about the area of focus. After considering the usefulness of these resources, teachers craft and implement solutions that they hypothesize will improve the area of need. The cycle concludes when teachers again gather and analyze evidence that is parallel to their baseline data, to determine the degree to which the implemented solutions led to change and to decide how to proceed. Teachers can fully repeat a cycle of inquiry in a new area of practice or alter and implement adjusted or entirely new solutions based on analyzed results.

Iterative Investigation is inspired by the tradition of action research. The Northeast and Islands Regional Educational Laboratory (LAB) at Brown University defines action research as a "disciplined inquiry done by a teacher with the intent that the research will inform and change his or her practices in the future" (Ferrance, 2000, p. 1). The LAB notes that action research was born in the 1940s and 1950s out of a belief that productive classroom change would be more likely if teachers studied and tried to systematically improve their instruction than if they simply read published studies about teaching and learning conducted by a formal education researcher.

Iterative Investigation maintains the key steps of action research— analyzing evidence to specify an area of instruction to change, learning and trying out new practices in an effort to improve, and documenting and analyzing evidence to determine the extent to which new practices led to improvements—and leverages the benefits of an online video platform to work with this evidence more efficiently and effectively.

An individual teacher can conduct an independent Iterative Investigation, or groups of teachers can work on a collaborative Iterative Investigation. Though teachers may be informed by and seek support from administrators, coaches, or even educational researchers, this learning strategy should be teacher-initiated and led. This strategy builds on Video Observation and Longer-Range Reflection, but is distinct from them in the degree to which it is teacher-driven, the way in which it leverages structured cycles of inquiry, and the level of specificity and complexity of challenges that can be addressed through it.

What are the benefits and impact of Iterative Investigation?

Iterative Investigation can afford several benefits, including improving classroom experiences and outcomes, deepening teacher skills, and promoting ownership of one's own professional learning. Teachers who use this learning strategy can strengthen their skill at spotting and interpreting areas for change in their classroom, locating relevant external research and supports for their own professional learning, and comparing multiple pieces of evidence. When teachers conduct investigations collaboratively, they can build habits of using peer analysis and feedback as a source of professional learning. And, more broadly, because this strategy requires teachers to gather and analyze evidence of their own practice at multiple points of time, it also helps improve their self-reflectiveness.

In addition to strengthening skills, Iterative Investigation can be very empowering for teachers. And while the structured cycle of inquiry provides a helpful scaffold to support teachers' efforts to improve, it also requires the initiative and judgment of the educator.

It puts teachers in the driver's seat and positions those in administrative or coaching roles as key supports to the process.

How do you implement Iterative Investigation?

PLANNING

- **Assemble educators who can serve as partners in Iterative Investigation.**

  Teachers benefit from having a partner to support them as they engage in this learning strategy. Administrators, coaches, mentors, peers, and even university faculty can partner with teachers. Consider creating and offering to teachers brief biographies of possible partners, highlighting their backgrounds and areas of expertise. Spend an hour sharing the opportunity with prospective partners, securing their agreement to make themselves available, and developing materials to share with teachers.

EXECUTION

Iterative Investigation should be a teacher-led learning strategy. Teachers should use the following steps, leaning on partners when they need support.

- **Analyze classroom evidence to define a challenge to investigate.**

  Teachers should review recently captured classroom footage to spot a challenge to tackle. The chosen challenge may be one that a peer, coach, or administrator has identified for improvement, but the teacher must also identify it as an area for growth and feel committed to a structured cycle of investigation to try and address it. The challenge should be an aspect of teaching and learning that, when addressed, will have a positive impact for students. Teachers should budget an amount of time at least equal to the total run time of the videos for review.

- **Select a partner to support their work.**

  This choice is up to each teacher, based on existing relation-ships or the match between a partner's areas of expertise and the challenge a teacher has decided to investigate. Teachers should spend about 30 minutes considering possible partners and making a decision about how to leverage the partner in the Iterative Investigation.

- **Record a baseline video of teaching and learning in the challenge area.**

  The teacher should capture video and select relevant clips that establish the baseline against which future evidence will be compared. Student work or data, student and family or guard-ian input, and teacher-recorded reflections can be added to the baseline video, if relevant. Teachers should record footage and budget one-and-a-half times the total run time of that footage to select clips to serve as baseline evidence of the area of challenge.

- **Consider establishing formal goals and metrics.**

  Some teachers find it helpful to clarify how they will know when they've made sufficient progress by setting goals—goals that might include a specific change in teacher or student action, like increasing the ratio of student vs. teacher talk time by 50 percent, or different achievement outcomes, like increasing children's independent reading stamina from 10-20 minutes. If teachers choose to set goals, they might find it useful to seek support from a partner. However, some teachers find goal-setting a time consuming process that doesn't add enough clarity to warrant the investment. Teachers should hold no more than an hour to clarify goals and metrics, if they choose to take this step in the process.

- **Identify resources for teacher learning to help develop a plan of action.**

  In this step of the cycle, teachers locate and engage with relevant resources. How have other educators approached this problem?

What are best practices in this area of instruction? What have formal education researchers concluded about what works? By finding people, examples, articles, blogs, or books that provide insight into these types of questions, teachers can learn from others before crafting a solution to test—or reinventing the wheel, so to speak.

Though teachers could spend endless amounts of time in this step, it's important to note that during Iterative Investigation, teachers learn the most from action. It's wise for teachers to limit themselves to a handful of hours (four to six hours, perhaps) to identify and consider external resources.

- **Develop and implement a plan of action.**
  In light of lessons learned from external resources, teachers develop a plan of action to address the challenge. That plan might involve efforts to improve relationships, content knowledge, pedagogy, curriculum, assessment, differentiation, and more. The plan might be relatively simple, such as making a set of adjustments to lesson plans or how the teacher implements them. Or it might be more complex, such as creating an entirely new structure for remediation or developing a multipronged approach to increasing student motivation.

  Once the teachers develop a plan, they implement the changes and sustain them over a long enough period of time to form new habits and determine impact, if any, with students. In implementation, teachers might reach out to a partner or coach for support, problem-solving, or feedback.

  The time needed for this step can vary significantly based on the simplicity or complexity of the plan. Teachers should consider limiting themselves to no more than three to four weeks of implementing a plan before they gather and analyze evidence of change.

- **Gather and analyze evidence to understand what's changed and why.**
  Teachers should gather evidence similar in type and volume
  to what they gathered at the baseline. If teachers have established formal goals, they can check the evidence against them.
  The purpose of this step is to understand what has changed
  for teacher and students and to consider what has led to or
  prohibited change. Teachers often find it helpful to complete
  this step with a partner, inviting others to view and comment
  on teaching clips. Teachers should record footage and budget
  one-and-a-half times the total run time of the videos to analyze
  clips for evidence of change.

- **In light of this analysis, determine implications for how to proceed.**
  In light of what they have learned through implementation and
  reflection, teachers might conclude that they haven't sufficiently
  addressed the challenge and return to tweak their plan of action.
  Or, they might conclude that they have improved as they hoped,
  and either move on to another area of challenge or a different
  professional learning strategy altogether. Regardless of their
  decision, it's useful to step back from the specific challenge and
  reflect on broader lessons learned from the cycle of Iterative
  Investigation. Budget around an hour to determine implications for how to proceed in light of the evidence of change and
  to reflect more broadly on lessons learned.

In total, Iterative Investigation can happen over several months or
across the entire school year. In the planning phase, an administrator or professional learning facilitator should plan to spend an hour
assembling a group of possible partners. The range of time teachers
need to implement Iterative Investigation can vary significantly,
depending on the depth of the challenge and the complexity of the
action plan. Teachers should spend about an hour defining a challenge
to investigate and select a partner. Beyond those execution steps, and

as a rough estimate, teachers should budget anywhere from 7-8 hours for simpler action plans to 20-25 hours for more complex ones.

ONLINE LESSON STUDY

Teachers and students in the Central School District are heading into the upcoming academic year with a new set of science standards. To provide targeted support to teachers, the district's science coordinator initiates grade-level specific lesson study groups and invites every school in the district to nominate one or two teachers to participate. These lesson study groups operate exclusively online, to allow teachers from across the district the necessary flexibility to collaborate with a broad set of their peers.

The second-grade lesson study group is preparing a science unit in which students investigate how and why land changes over time. The group has committed to collaboratively plan lessons and to share videos of their practice with one another. In the virtual kick-off meeting, teachers decide they want to focus their work on the ways students listen to and consider the perspectives of peers, understand weathering and erosion, and use specific engineering practices to design, test, and evaluate solutions to soil erosion.

With these aims in mind, teachers spend the next week gathering and uploading resources that might support their lesson planning, including the new standards, a module from their district's science curriculum, and videos illustrating weathering and erosion. The next two planning meetings happen over video conference using shared planning documents online. In these meetings, the team collaborates to design one lesson from the unit, discussing in-depth the purpose of the activities within the lesson and what they hope to see or hear from students during each one. At the end of the second planning meeting, one teacher in the group agrees to record and share footage of her implementation of the lesson.

Two weeks later, the team regroups in an afterschool video conference. Each member has spent time viewing and commenting on the volunteer teacher's video. Those comments focus on student ideas, thought processes, and habits of discussion and collaboration with peers. The team spends time discussing the lesson design decisions that were more and less helpful to students, given the larger goals the teachers established. For example, teachers note the usefulness of landform models in helping students visualize how erosion happens, but contrast that with the misconceptions students held about how quickly erosion occurs. They also describe how students who entered the lesson with strongly-held conceptions about why erosion happens dominated small group discussions.

The meeting concludes with the teachers agreeing to redesign the research lesson, using a different set of erosion phenomena, to try to help students better understand erosion timelines, as well as listen to and consider their peers' perspectives.

What is Online Lesson Study?

Online Lesson Study involves a group of educators working collaboratively to focus on specific goals for student learning and well-being, deeply examine instructional materials relevant to those aims, design and teach a lesson while observers analyze students, and discuss the results. Online Lesson Study allows educators who want to implement the Japanese tradition of lesson study (or lesson research) to do so via video. The centerpiece of the Japanese tradition is a co-planned research lesson which is observed, analyzed, and improved on by a team of educators. This professional learning strategy is arguably the most complex and time intensive of those featured in this playbook.

In Japan, lesson study is one of the primary professional learning strategies for both pre-service and practicing teachers. It is credited with helping Japanese schools transform their mathematics and science instruction, particularly at the elementary level (CBS, 2010). Educators in the United States began to experiment with lesson study in the 1990s, when several researchers, including Catherine Lewis at Mills College, Makoto Yoshida at the University of Chicago, and James Stigler at UCLA, among others, began examining the practice at work in Japanese schools, sharing their analyses through research articles, books, and conferences, and supporting U.S. schools to implement it.

In light of guidance from the Lesson Study Group at Mills College ("What is Lesson Study?" 2015) and from Akihiko Takahashi and Thomas McDougal (2016), Online Lesson Study should involve:

- discussion of the broader aims of education for children, like fostering motivation or kindness, and selection of one to work on in lesson study;
- discussion of the narrower goals in specific content-areas or within units—such as understanding ratio concepts and using ratio reasoning to solve problems in math, or developing a topic with facts and details in informative writing—and selecting one learning goal that has been challenging for students;
- collaborative design of a classroom "research lesson" that intends to help students progress toward both broader educational aims and narrower content learning goals, by studying standards, curriculum, and other instructional materials, like math manipulatives or specific texts;
- implementation of that lesson publicly, via video, while observers interpret students' responses, including their thinking, engagement, and interactions with one another; and
- discussion of the analysis of student responses, in order to deepen understanding of teaching and learning and to identify implications for the design of future lessons.

All of the focusing techniques outlined in chapter 3 can be useful in supporting teachers' analysis of the research lesson video. Teachers can spot patterns of student behavior that are meaningfully helping or hindering student learning. They can break down instruction into component parts and interpret the effects of each component on student learning. And they can toggle back and forth between the lesson plan and the footage of that plan being implemented to compare teachers' hypotheses about what would facilitate student learning with evidence that indicates whether their planned instruction actually succeeded. Finally, because they work in collaboration with their peers, they can discuss each other's perspectives on the evidence they've viewed.

To learn more about the Japanese approach to lesson study, we suggest "A Lesson is like a Swiftly Flowing River: How Research Lessons Improve Japanese Education" by Catherine Lewis and Ineko Tsuchida (1999) and *Lesson Study: A Handbook for Teacher-Led Instructional Change* by Catherine Lewis (2002).

What are the benefits and impact of Online Lesson Study?

The potential benefits of Online Lesson Study are significant and extend farther than the teaching and learning that happens within any single research lesson. Catherine Lewis et al. (2001, p.19) explain that lesson study builds "underlying pathways to instructional improvement," by increasing teachers' knowledge of content and of instruction; improving their ability to observe students; fostering stronger professional learning communities; helping teachers see connections between daily instruction and longer-term aims for students; improving teachers' motivation and ability to develop professionally; and increasing the quality of lesson plans within a school.

Bradley Ermeling and Genevieve Graff-Ermeling are two American educators who engaged in lesson study as ninth-grade English teachers in Japan. They describe how their participation in lesson study helped them strengthen their skills at crafting a coherent lesson storyline and justifying every aspect of their lesson design (Ermeling and Graff-Ermeling, 2014). They also note how rigorously they began to examine and use evidence through every stage of lesson study. Adapting lesson study to an online platform further amplifies this benefit, as evidence can be easily uploaded, examined, and organized.

Similar to Video Rounds, evolving lesson study to an online format reduces the logistical complexity for schools or organizations that want to implement it. Rather than having to locate coverage for every classroom whose teacher is observing the research lesson, administrators can allow teachers view uploaded footage when convenient. And while post-lesson discussion can happen in-person when students are not in the building, it can also happen online. The virtual nature of this strategy allows other educators with needed expertise to participate, even if they are not physically close to the school. The increased flexibility with which teachers and other partners can collaborate in Online Lesson Study helps make this learning strategy work for many schools.

How do you implement Online Lesson Study?

PLANNING

- **Initiate Online Lesson Study as a professional learning strategy and identify participants.**

  Online Lesson Study can be initiated by teachers, administrators, or professional developers. Determine who will participate in Online Lesson Study, including specific teachers and any other educators who might contribute. Teachers in Japan benefit from the inclusion of a "knowledgeable other," someone who brings expertise in the particular content area, in instructional design, or in the psychology of learning to different steps of the work. Consider whether such people might participate in some or all phases of the work alongside teachers. Plan to spend an hour on this step.

EXECUTION

- **Online Lesson Study group meets to identify a research theme.**
  In the meeting that launches Online Lesson Study, teachers determine a theme to govern the cycle. To do so, they look at evidence relative to the broader aims of education for children and the narrower goals of specific content areas—evidence like student work and aggregated data, footage of students working in class, and survey data. Group members should plan to spend about an hour identifying a research theme.

- **Group members design a research lesson.**
  Teachers collaboratively design a classroom research lesson related to the identified theme. To do so, they examine learning standards, curriculum, and other instructional materials, like manipulatives, technology, texts, and tools.

  The research lesson need not be designed from scratch. In fact, teachers in Japan begin by closely studying lessons from their national curriculum. If teachers begin with existing lessons, their work is to study those carefully and determine any adjustments that might better serve holistic purposes of education for children and the specific academic goals of a disciplinary area or unit of instruction.

  When lesson planning, teachers also consider the evidence they hope to see from students during every learning activity, to indicate the degree to which students should be progressing across the lesson.

  The work of this step can happen in one meeting or be stretched across several meetings. Plan to spend two to three hours on this work.

- **Determine which group member will record and share footage of the lesson being implemented with students.**

  Someone from the Online Lesson Study group should volunteer to implement and record the research lesson and share it with group members. Plan to make this decision in the concluding 5-10 minutes of a lesson design meeting.

- **Volunteer teacher implements and records research lesson.**

  The volunteer team member teaches the research lesson to his or her students. Because observers are going to focus so much of their analysis on student thinking, interactions, and engagement, it's particularly important to ensure recording devices and microphones are placed appropriately. Press record as class begins and capture the lesson in its entirety.

- **Volunteer shares footage of lesson and any related evidence.**

  The volunteer shares footage of the lesson with lesson study team members. Unlike other learning strategies, it is best to share footage from the entire lesson. The teacher should consider sharing other artifacts of student thinking, like sample work. Plan to spend about 10 minutes gathering and sharing any additional artifacts, alongside video.

- **Other group members view footage and analyze students.**

  Other members of the Online Lesson Study group watch the lesson and leave comments throughout, striving to interpret the effect of the lesson design on student thinking, behavior, and engagement. Plan to spend roughly double the runtime of the lesson video for this work.

- **Prepare for post-lesson meeting by designating people to play various roles and determining a meeting format.**

  The team will benefit from having someone to serve as moderator and note taker during the meeting. If the Online Lesson Study group includes knowledgeable others as part of the process, the post-lesson meeting is an important phase for them to participate.

  Determine a format for the meeting. Vibrant discussion can take place in comment threads within the video, in a video conference, in-person, or in a combination of those methods. Budget approximately 15 minutes to prepare for the post-lesson meeting.

- **In the meeting, have evidence-based discussion centered around student behaviors, ideas, and learning rather than on teacher performance.**

  Some teams find it useful for the volunteer teacher to open the meeting by sharing his or her observations about those aspects of the plan that supported students toward the identified goals and those that were less successful. Other colleagues then contribute their ideas, with the moderator encouraging them to cite evidence from the lesson, to extend one another's ideas, and to raise divergent interpretations of what they observed. Plan to spend 60-90 minutes discussing analysis of the research lesson.

- **Conclude the meeting by reflecting broadly and identifying implications.**

  Each team member can summarize what he or she has learned about teaching and learning broadly, as a result of observing the research lesson and participating in the post-lesson discussion. They can also determine whether to redesign the research lesson and engage in another cycle of observation and discussion, or to identify implications for the design of future lessons. Finally, they can identify possible areas of research for future lesson study cycles. This work can happen within the post-lesson meeting.

In total, one round of Online Lesson Study can happen over several weeks and be repeated as often as desired across a school year. In Japan, the work of one cycle is typically spread across five weeks and is an ongoing feature of teacher development (Takahashi and McDougal, 2016). The facilitator should budget an hour to initiate and prepare for Online Lesson Study.

For each round of Online Lesson Study, group members should plan to spend around seven hours, while the volunteer teacher should budget an additional 10 minutes or so to gather resources and share the research lesson with others. The facilitator of Online Lesson Study should budget an additional fifteen minutes to prepare for the post-lesson meeting.

AFTERWORD

VIDEO CHANGES EVERYTHING

Jim Knight

Jim Knight is a research associate at University of Kansas Center for Research on Learning, senior partner of the Instructional Coaching Group, and president of Impact Research Lab. He has spent more than a decade studying instructional coaching and has written several books on the topic.

I n the past three decades, three technological innovations have transformed professional development in U.S. schools. The first two are obvious. The computer and the Internet have dramatically increased every educators' creative potential while putting the world of knowledge at everyone's fingertips. The third innovation is less obvious: video recordings from handheld technology such as smartphones and tablets. We have known about the power of video for decades, with studies at Stanford University in the 1970s showing how helpful it can be for teachers to video record and view their lessons. The technology used to be too disruptive, difficult, and expensive to use, but now almost everyone has a phone in their pocket that they can easily and quickly use to video record their lessons. Video changes everything.

In this chapter, I will summarize what I learned about video while writing *Focus on Teaching: Using Video for High-Impact Instruction* (2014) and from interviews and conversations I've had since the book was published. My comments will be organized around three simple questions: Why? Why not? How?

Why?

Video can dramatically accelerate professional learning in schools. A primary reason is that video helps educators get a clear picture of reality, which should be an important point of departure for any learning – to move forward, we need to know where we are.

My colleagues and I at The Impact Research Lab have found that video is so important because people don't have a clear picture of what it looks like when they do what they do. Unfortunately, as I pointed out in *Focus on Teaching*, we all see reality through various perceptual errors (such as confirmation bias and habituation) and, therefore, don't see reality clearly. Video cuts through these perceptual errors and reveals reality for what it is.

Athletes have known for years about the power of video. Likely almost every middle school football team in the U.S. watches video of their games. Now, educators are realizing the power of video, and video is one of the most rapidly growing tools for professional learning in schools.

There are many other reasons why video is powerful. When teachers see a recording of their lesson, they are often more motivated to change than would be likely without a clear picture of reality. Watching video of a lesson also helps educators identify more accurately where they need to improve (either by doing more of what is working or less of what's not working). Additionally, video makes it easier for instructional coaches, principals, and educators to talk about video because it is objective and not subjective. Finally, when a teacher pushes the red button and records a lesson, she is committing to doing something to make classes even better. In short, video moves schools from a culture of talk to a culture of action.

Why Not?

Despite the obvious benefits of video, the most common question I am asked about its use is, "How do we get people to do it?" The simple truth is that few people like to see themselves on video. Most of us don't like the way we look on video. I have interviewed many people after they have watched video of themselves teaching or communicating, and so far no one has said, "Wow! I'm younger and thinner than I thought." The reality is that people we see at the movies and on our various screens are fictional – someone took hours to fix their hair and do their makeup; the lighting is perfect; and the camera lens is worth $30,000. It shouldn't come as a surprise, therefore, that the image we see of ourselves on our iPad, recorded under fluorescent lights in the classroom, doesn't look as a great as a movie star. However, the good news is that after seeing themselves a few times, most people are able to look beyond their own image to focus on the more important aspects of video. If people can persist, they will move beyond their concerns about appearance, and really start powerful learning.

People also hesitate to watch video because they are afraid of what they will see. Video can threaten our identity because it shows us as we are, not as we think we are. In *Thanks for the Feedback* (2014), Douglas Stone and Sheila Heen define identity as "the story we tell ourselves about who we are and what the future holds for us" (p. 2). Video often forces us to rethink our story of who we are, and that is not an easy task. However, staying comfortably unaware of what it looks like when we do what we do is not a good alternative, either. As for most learning, sometimes to get better we need to step outside of our comfort zone.

But perhaps the main reason people don't use video is that they don't know who will see it and how it will be used. If people don't trust their coach, administrator, district leaders, or the people on their team, they likely aren't going to want use video. We have found that video use varies more by school than it does by person. In other words, when people feel they can trust those around them, they don't hesitate to use video, but when they don't feel trust, they rarely want to be recorded.

In *Better Conversations: Coaching Ourselves to Be More Credible, Caring, and Connected* (2015), I identify five variables that affect whether or not people trust each other – character, reliability, warmth, competence, and stewardship. If the teachers in a school are hesitant to use video, leaders should consider which variable they need to address to create a culture of trust. Without trust, there likely won't be much productive use of video.

How?

Our research has shown us that video can be a power tool for personal and professional improvement. In *Better Conversations,* I describe how video can help people learn and internalize 10 habits that will help anyone be a better communicator. Our schools, I like to say, are only as good as our conversations, and video provides a powerful way for schools to quickly improve how people interact. Many free tools are available to improve the way we communicate at https://resources. corwin.com/knightbetterconversations .

In *The Impact Cycle: What Instructional Coaches Should Do to Foster Powerful Improvements in Teaching* (2018), I describe how video can be used as a part of instructional coaching. We have come to see video as a critical tool for helping us partner with teachers to set goals and monitor progress toward goals. In fact, most coaches I've worked with who use video say, "I don't know how I was able to do coaching before I used video."

Finally, in *Focus on Teaching*, I write about other ways video can be used by individuals, coaches, teams, and principals, and I also address a number of practical concerns about how to use video. In addition, I include videos of teachers, coaches, teams, and principals using video to promote professional learning.

No matter how well intended, video likely won't be embraced unless it is implemented with care. If leaders rush implementation of video, they can stir up fear and resentment and, ultimately, the good intentions of promoting powerful learning can backfire. In *Focus on Teaching*, I identify five conditions necessary to create a flourishing coaching program: establish trust, make participation a choice, focus on intrinsic motivation and safety, establish clear boundaries, and walk the talk with leaders watching themselves on video.

In summary, the use of video is growing in schools for good reasons. Video can improve a school's capacity for learning by improving the kind of conversations taking place in schools, and video can help teachers, coaches, teams, and principals be much more effective as they work to foster better teaching for better learning. When implemented with care, video can be a power tool for learning. Implemented carelessly, video can make things worse by engendering resistance. Leaders are wise to take the time to share video effectively. That likely means starting by recording themselves before asking others to do the same.

APPENDICES

APPENDIX A

PLAY-BY-PLAY SUMMARY

S T R A T E G Y   1

CLASSROOM TOUR

Teachers narrate a walk-through of their empty classroom or workspace, highlighting why and how the physical space and materials are organized to support student learning.

TOTAL TIME:

one to several days

HOW TO IMPLEMENT

PLANNING

- Facilitator spends up to 10 minutes setting guidelines.
- Teachers spend 5 minutes deciding what to capture.

EXECUTION

- Teachers record a 2-5 minute narrated walk-through.
- Colleagues spend 5 minutes watching the tour and providing feedback.

HOW TO EXTEND

- Conduct a "micro" Classroom Tour by featuring one small part of the physical space, such as the classroom library, stations or centers, displays that honor student culture, lab set-ups, etc.
- Involve students from the previous year's classroom in narrating the tour, to highlight student perspectives on the physical space.
- Share the video with students and families in advance of the first day of school to help orient students.

STRATEGY 2

SELF-INTERVIEW

A teacher records a video describing his or her goals for individual students, an entire class, or their own professional growth, as well as why those goals matter to student learning and well-being.

TOTAL TIME:

one to several days

HOW TO IMPLEMENT

PLANNING

- Facilitator spends about 10 minutes offering guidance for Self-interview.

EXECUTION

- Teachers record a Self-Interview that is 10 minutes or less.
- Peers and coaches spend an amount of time equal to the runtime of the video footage to view and offer affirming, clarifying, or probing feedback.

HOW TO EXTEND THIS LEARNING STRATEGY

- Ask a colleague to conduct an interview, rather than using the Self-Interview format.
- Ask students to share their aspirations, interests, preferences for learning, strengths, and challenges. Have teachers analyze this evidence using Self-Interview to support their instructional decision making.

S T R A T E G Y   3

EXAMPLE ANALYSIS

Teachers independently analyze a video clip of instruction to deepen their understanding of what constitutes quality teaching and learning, so that they might apply that knowledge within their own practice.

TOTAL TIME:
several days or weeks

HOW TO IMPLEMENT

PLANNING

- Facilitator spends an hour selecting example video, offering guidance for teachers' analysis, and deciding whether to include discussion as part of implementation.

EXECUTION

- Facilitator selects example footage; length of clips can vary.
- Teachers spend one-and-a-half times the runtime of the example video to watch and analyze footage.
- Facilitator spends one-and-a-half times the total runtime of the example video to read and consider each teacher's analysis.
- If included, facilitator and teachers spend 30 minutes in discussion.

HOW TO EXTEND

- Instead of sharing one example video, ask teachers to analyze and compare multiple videos. This set can include examples and nonexamples.

Strategy 4

PRE-TEACH

Teachers record themselves rehearsing portions of upcoming instruction in order to refine their practice before implementing with students.

TOTAL TIME:

one or several days

HOW TO IMPLEMENT

PLANNING

- Facilitator spends 10 minutes deciding what teachers should Pre-Teach and whether to use the solo or role-play version of the strategy.

EXECUTION

- Teachers record a segment of instruction that can range from 90 seconds to 7 minutes in length. Other teachers may play the role of students.
- Teachers, peers, and facilitator spend one-and-a-half times the total run-time of the video clip to analyze and discuss asynchronously.
- If synchronous discussion is selected, budget an additional 20 minutes.

HOW TO EXTEND

- Teachers can view the Pre-Teach video alongside implementation footage to compare and contrast.

STRATEGY 5

VIDEO OBSERVATION

Teachers capture footage to determine the current state of teaching and learning and, independently or with a partner, determine next steps to support continued professional growth.

TOTAL TIME:
several days to two weeks

HOW TO IMPLEMENT

PLANNING

- Teachers spend 30 minutes reflecting on professional development goals and the current state their classroom.
- If choosing Partner-Supported Reflection, teacher and partner align on the goals and incoming beliefs about the classroom.

EXECUTION

- Teachers record video of their instruction. If choosing Partner-Supported Reflection, either teachers or partners can select segments of instruction for analysis.
- Teachers and any reflection partners spend roughly one-and-a-half times the runtime of the chosen video clip to view and analyze.
- If selected, teachers and partners spend 30 minutes discussing the teacher's analysis.

HOW TO EXTEND

- Partner-Supported Reflection can be evolved to more formal cycles of improvement by establishing improvement goals, engaging in professional learning, and capturing and analyzing evidence of teacher growth.

STRATEGY 6

SKILL BUILDING SEQUENCE

Teachers watch and analyze an example video that models a specific skill, enact that specific skill in a video of their own, and share footage with a coach, in order to provide a checkpoint on their skill development.

TOTAL TIME:

one to several weeks

HOW TO IMPLEMENT

PLANNING

- Facilitator spends 30-60 minutes identifying a targeted learning skill for a group of teachers, selecting an example video which highlights a targeted skill, and designing a structured analysis.

EXECUTION

- Teachers implement the target skill and capture 5-15 minutes of new classroom footage.
- Teachers spend roughly double the runtime of videos to analyze the example footage and to reflect on evidence of their own implementation.
- Facilitator spends roughly double the runtime of videos to analyze teacher's implementation footage.

HOW TO EXTEND

- Instead of having teachers analyze an example video, have them analyze a live model seen during an in-person professional development day. They can then return to their classrooms to implement the skill themselves and capture footage.

STRATEGY 7

VIDEO LEARNING COMMUNITY

Teachers view, analyze, and discuss footage of one another's classrooms in order to fuel collective improvement of the community members.

TOTAL TIME:
several months to across the entire school year

HOW TO IMPLEMENT

PLANNING

- Facilitator spends 60-90 minutes initiating and launching the community.
- Teachers spend 10 minutes considering the parameters of the community.

EXECUTION

- Teachers capture 5 minutes of instruction.
- Teachers spend double the total run-time of the videos under review.
- Teachers spend one to two hours for discussion.

HOW TO EXTEND

- Secure footage from external sources for teachers to analyze, for some or all of the VLC meetings.

VIRTUAL WALK-THROUGH

Observers view short segments of lesson-length video footage, aiming to identify trends in teaching and learning across classrooms and to provide accurate and specific feedback to teachers.

> **TOTAL TIME:**
> *approximately one month*

HOW TO IMPLEMENT

PLANNING

- Facilitator spends 90 minutes determining observers, establishing purposes with teachers, and setting a schedule for analyzing shared videos.
- Teachers spend 10 minutes setting their schedules for capturing and sharing video.

EXECUTION

- Teachers record and share footage of entire lessons.
- For each classroom observed, hold at least 10 minutes to view and analyze footage and to follow-up with teachers.
- Reflection at the end of a round of Virtual Walk-Through will take observers 30-60 minutes.

HOW TO EXTEND

- Virtual Walk-Through can be refocused as a skill-building opportunity for teachers to correctly spot the prioritized look-fors and listen-fors across a broader cross-section of teachers, alongside more experienced observers.

STRATEGY 9

VIDEO ROUNDS

A team of educators view and discuss video clips from multiple classrooms to identify and learn from trends across a school or system.

TOTAL TIME:

several weeks or months

HOW TO IMPLEMENT

PLANNING

- Facilitator spends four to five hours preparing to launch Video Rounds.

EXECUTION

- Teachers capture video of their instruction.
- Video Rounds members spend double the total runtime of the videos under review analyzing footage and approximately five hours in discussion and action.
- Facilitator spends five to eight hours preparing for, supporting, and taking action coming out of discussions about analyzed videos.

HOW TO EXTEND

- Consider limiting or expanding who is asked to serve on the Video Rounds team. For example, limit membership to administrators or school leadership team members or expand to include students and families or guardians.

STRATEGY 10

LONGER-RANGE REFLECTION

Teachers examine a recent video alongside previously reviewed videos and commentary in order to identify evidence of change in practice over time and to discern the contributing factors.

TOTAL TIME:
several days

HOW TO IMPLEMENT

PLANNING

- Facilitator spends about an hour determining a time period for reflection and providing teachers guidance.

EXECUTION

- Teachers select previously and recently recorded footage to view.
- Teachers spend at least one-and-a-half times the total run time of the videos for review.

HOW TO EXTEND

- Consider using Longer-Range Reflection within the Partner-Supported Reflection version of Video Observation.

ITERATIVE INVESTIGATION

Teachers engage in a structured cycle of inquiry within their own classrooms in order to improve instruction, student and teacher experiences, and student outcomes.

TOTAL TIME:
several months to across the entire school year

HOW TO IMPLEMENT

PLANNING

- Facilitator spends an hour assembling a group of possible partners to support teachers in the investigation.

EXECUTION

- Teachers examine videos of routine instruction to define a challenge. Then, they record baseline and post-investigation videos to identify change.
- Teachers should budget an amount of time at least equal to the total run time of the initial videos, in order to define a challenge, and one-and-a-half times the total run time of footage, to analyze baseline and post-investigation clips.
- Teachers spend between 10 to 25 hours to implement the investigation.

S T R A T E G Y   1 2

ONLINE LESSON STUDY

A group of educators work collaboratively to focus on specific goals
for student learning and well-being,
deeply examine instructional materials relevant to those aims, design and
teach a lesson while observers analyze
students, and discuss the results.

TOTAL TIME:

several weeks

HOW TO IMPLEMENT

PLANNING

- Facilitator spends an hour initiating
  the learning strategy.

EXECUTION

- Volunteer teacher records footage of
  the entire research lesson.
- Teachers spend about seven hours
  designing and debriefing the research
  lesson.
- Facilitator spends an additional 15
  minutes preparing for the post-lesson
  meeting.

GUIDANCE FOR RECORDING AND SHARING CLASSROOM VIDEO

We live in a world with high-quality video cameras built into devices we use every day. The ease of accessing devices like smartphones, tablets, or laptops has removed many of the technical barriers of the past—barriers that once prevented video-based learning initiatives from working at scale across schools or organizations. To best support teachers, it helps to make decisions related to recording and sharing classroom video.

What device should teachers use?

Make sure the capture devices are common and easy to use. A device that requires a check-out from the media center and 20 minutes of setup is not as ideal as a camera that is readily available on a device already in the classroom. In other words, while a camera robot might be a nice-to-have, it's certainly not a necessity. Make the barrier to pushing record low.

The place to focus energy is on the audio capture, as the video will likely be "good enough" regardless of your device. Most devices only have a pinhole microphone, which is fine for a phone call or video conference, but may leave something to be desired in classroom environments.

If the school already has recording devices, consider supplementing them with external microphones that can plug into the headphone jack or charging port. If the school is buying dedicated devices, consider a video camera with a substantial microphone—one designed for recording in noisy environments.

Who and what should teachers capture on video?

Decide who to capture (teachers, students, or both) and in what settings (whole group, small group, or one-on-one interactions), depending on the purpose of the professional learning strategy being used. Jim Knight (2014) suggests teachers point the camera toward themselves when trying to understand or improve a specific element of their instruction (such as the types of questions they pose, the amount of teacher talk vs. student talk, and the consistency of their student corrections) and toward students when trying to understand or improve specific student behaviors (such as their time on task, their authentic engagement, or the quality and thoughtfulness of their responses).

Consult school or organizational policies to ensure you secure the appropriate permissions to obtain and share classroom footage.

Of what quality should video be?

Teachers do not need to share their "best of" instructional footage. Instead, they should capture the everyday reality of classroom life. Additionally, teachers do not need to share only clips that meet a high bar for production quality. Having some video is always better than having none, even if there are moments where the camera isn't close enough to see what's written on the board or hear a particular student's comment.

How much footage should teachers capture and share?

Advise teachers to record whatever amount of footage they like. If teachers want to get into the habit of regularly viewing lesson-length videos of their classrooms, it will most likely help them improve their practice. It may also be simpler for teachers to press record at the start of a lesson and not worry about the video camera again until the lesson is over. Remember: it is always possible to edit footage down after it is captured.

When deciding how much video to share, guide teachers to consider it as parallel to how much time an observer might need to spend to understand the topic at hand. For some topics, a video as short as 90 seconds might be sufficient, while other topics might require observers to see more instruction. In general, sharing 10-12 minutes of instruction usually provides enough evidence to analyze and work with, though shorter clips also have value. A narrow 3-5 minute segment can also help viewers focus and deepen their analysis—and may be more realistic for teachers with many items on the to-do list.

With whom should teachers share?

Depending on the specific strategy for professional learning, there may be reason to keep video private. In other cases, teachers might share footage only with a coach. Given the value of collaborative discussion of video evidence, encourage teachers to share their clips widely with peers across the school or organization when appropriate.

How long should viewers spend analyzing videos?

The amount of time necessary to analyze a video clip will vary based on the length of the clip, the depth of analysis required, and the complexity of the instruction featured. In-depth analysis of five minutes of student discussion will take longer than it does to review five minutes of a classroom tour.

It is important to share realistic time estimates with those analyzing videos, so they can plan appropriately. Within each strategy we offer suggested time needed based on video length. For videos that require basic analysis of a relatively simple instructional practice, we advise spending roughly equal the runtime of the video clip. For footage that requires deeper analysis of more complicated instruction, we recommend spending one-and-a-half times the total runtime of the clip. For video that requires the deepest analysis of more complicated practices or asynchronous discussion within threaded comment, we suggest spending double the runtime of the footage. You'll have to bring your own judgment to bear to finalize time estimates for video analysis, but these general rules should help.

FRAMEWORK FOR FACILITATION OF VIDEO-BASED DISCUSSION

ORIENTING GROUP TO THE VIDEO ANALYSIS TASK

FACILITATION MOVE	DEFINITION	EXAMPLE
Launching	Pose general prompts to elicit participant ideas	"So, what did you notice? What stood out to you?" "What were interesting mathematical moments or interchanges in the video?"
Contextualizing	Provide additional information about the classroom context and mathematics lesson	"This was a lesson on 2-digit multiplication, and you were working the partial products method."

SUSTAINING AN INQUIRY STANCE

FACILITATION MOVE	DEFINITION	EXAMPLE
Highlighting	Direct attention to note-worthy student ideas in the videos	"So it seems like we're all pretty interested in what Tyrone did here. What did he mean by one-fourth equals 25 and one-half is 50?"
Lifting up	Identify an important idea that a participant raised in the discussion for further discussion	"I think you were bringing up the idea that maybe they understood what met goal exactly meant, but they had this way of thinking that it wasn't each student that got to 50 but rather collectively."
Pressing	Prompt participants to explain their reasoning and/or elaborate on their ideas	"You said there was a lot she had to do there, can you piece apart for me all the things you think she had to do?"
Offering an explanation	Provide an interpretation of an event, interaction, or mathematical idea, from a stance of inquiry	"I was thinking that he might have looked at his partner's cards and added the numbers on their two together. That might be why he said 51."
Countering	Offer an alternative point of view	"You could be right but I was thinking that the sticks and dots weren't really helping Dante. He doesn't arrive at the correct answer . . ."
Clarifying	Restate and revoice to ensure common under-standing of an idea	"So you're saying no, she doesn't really think it's ten?"

MAINTAINING A FOCUS ON THE VIDEO

FACILITATION MOVE	DEFINITION	EXAMPLE
Redirecting	Shift the discussion to maintain focus on the task of video analysis	"Can I just bring us back to the video for a second?"
Pointing to evidence	Contribute substantively to the conversation, using evidence to reason about teaching and learning with video	"Well, what did Jerome say earlier? . . . because I'm wondering if maybe she's using what he said earlier to help her try to figure this out. So, if we look on the page before . . ."
Connecting ideas	Make connections between ideas raised in the discussion	"So it's similar to what Tom was doing." "Do you have any predictions about what your students would do if they were given this problem?"

SUPPORTING GROUP COLLABORATION

FACILITATION MOVE	DEFINITION	EXAMPLE
Standing back	Allow the group members time to discuss an issue	Not interjecting when the group is exploring an idea
Distributing participation	Invite participants to share different ideas based on who is (and is not) participating	"Lisa, it looked like you wanted to say something . . ." "What do others think about that idea?"
Validating participant ideas	Confirm and support participant contributions	"That's really hard." "That could make sense, too. That could be another interpretation."

REFERENCES AND FURTHER READING

Aguilar, E. (2013). *The art of coaching: effective strategies for school transformation.* San Francisco: Jossey-Bass.

Aguilar, E. (2014, February 26). What Happens When Instructional Rounds Go District-Wide? Retrieved from https://www.edutopia.org/blog/instructional-rounds-distrct-wide-benefits-elena-aguilar

Allen, D. W., & Eve, A. W. (1968). Microteaching. *Theory Into Practice, 7*(5), 181-185. doi:10.1080/00405846809542153

Allen, J. P., Pianta, R. C., Gregory, A., Mikami, A. Y., & Lun, J. (2011). An Interaction-Based Approach to Enhancing Secondary School Instruction and Student Achievement. *Science, 333*(6045), 1034-1037. doi:10.1126/science.1207998

Ball, D., & Cohen, D. (1999). Developing practice, developing practitioners: Toward a practice-based theory of professional education. In L. Darling-Hammond & G. Sykes (Eds.), *Teaching as the learning profession: handbook of policy and practice* (pp. 3-32). San Francisco: Jossey-Bass .

Blomberg, G., Renkl, A., Sherin, M. G., Borko, H., & Seidel, T. (2013). Five research-based heuristics for using video in pre-service teacher education. Journal for educational research online, 5(1), 90.

Borko, H., Jacobs, J., Eiteljorg, E., & Pittman, M. E. (2008). Video as a tool for fostering productive discussions in mathematics professional development. *Teaching and Teacher Education, 24*(2), 417-436. doi:10.1016/j.tate.2006.11.012

Borko, H., Koellner, K., Jacobs, J., & Seago, N. (2010). Using video representations of teaching in practice-based professional development programs. *Zdm, 43*(1), 175-187. doi:10.1007/s11858-010-0302-5

Bryan, L. A., & Recesso, A. (2006). Promoting reflection among science student teachers using a web-based video analysis tool. *Journal of Computing in Teacher Education, 23*(1), 31-39.

CBS. (2010, September 29). Japan's Lesson Study. Retrieved from https://www.youtube.com/watch?v=0xgko79kO94

City, E. A. (2011). Learning from instructional rounds. *Educational Leadership, 69*(2), 36-41.

City, E. A., Elmore, R. F., Fiarman, S. E., & Teitel, L. (2009). *Instructional rounds in education: a network approach to improving teaching and learning.* Cambridge (Massachusetts): Harvard Education Press.

Cohen, S. R. (2004). *Teachers professional development and the elementary mathematics classroom: bringing understanding to light.* Mahwah, NJ: Lawrence Erlbaum.

Cuthrell, K., Steadman, S. C., Stapleton, J., & Hodge, E. (2016). Developing Expertise: Using Video to Hone Teacher Candidates' Classroom Observation Skills. *The New Educator, 12*(1), 5-27. doi:10.1080/1547688x.2015.1113349

David, J. (2008). What research says about...Classroom walk-throughs. *Educational Leadership, 65*(4), 81-82.

Del Prete, T. (1997). The rounds model of professional development. *From the Inside, 1*(1), 12-13.

Downey, C. J., Steffy, B., English, F. W., Frase, L. E., & Poston, W. K. (2004). *The three-minute classroom walk-through: changing school supervisory practice one teacher at a time.* Thousand Oaks, CA: Corwin.

DuFour, R. (2004). What is a professional learning community? *Educational Leadership, 61*(8), 6-11.

DuFour, R., & Eaker, R. E. (1998). *Professional learning communities at work: best practices for enhancing student achievement.* Bloomington, IN: National Education Service.

DuFour, R. (2006). *Learning by doing: a handbook for professional learning communities at work.* Bloomington, IN: Solution Tree Press.

Dweck, C. S. (2006). *Mindset: The new psychology of success.* Random House Incorporated.

Elish-Piper, L., & L'Allier, S. K. (2011). Examining the Relationship between Literacy Coaching and Student Reading Gains in Grades K–3. *The Elementary School Journal, 112*(1), 83-106. doi:10.1086/660685

Ermeling, B. A., & Graff-Ermeling, G. (2014). Learning to learn from teaching: a first-hand account of lesson study in Japan. *International journal for lesson and learning studies, 3*(2), 170-191.

Ferrance, E. (2000). Action research. *Northeast and Islands Regional Educational Laboratory at Brown University.*

Grossman, P., Compton, C., Igra, D., Ronfeldt, M., Shahan, E., & Williamson, P. (2009). Teaching practice: A cross-professional perspective. *Teachers College Record, 111*(9), 2055-2100.

Grossman, P., Hammerness, K., & Mcdonald, M. (2009). Redefining teaching, re-imagining teacher education. *Teachers and Teaching, 15*(2), 273-289. doi:10.1080/13540600902875340

Hattie, J. A. (2008). *Visible learning: a synthesis of over 800 meta-analyses relating to achievement.* London: Routledge.

Heifetz, R. A., & Linsky, M. (2002). *Leadership on the line: staying alive through the dangers of leading.* Harvard Business Press.

Hunzicker, J. (2011). Teacher learning through National Board candidacy: A conceptual model. *Teacher Education Quarterly, 38*(3), 191-209.

Jacobs, J., Borko, H., & Koellner, K. (2009). The power of video as a tool for professional development and research: Examples from the Problem-Solving Cycle. *The power of video studies in investigating teaching and learning in the classroom,* 259-273.

Joyce, B., & Showers, B. (1989). *Student Achievement Through Staff Development.* New York: Longman.

Kachur, D., Stout, J., & Edwards, C. L. (2010). *Classroom walkthroughs to improve teaching and learning.* Larchmont, NY: Eye on Education.

Kersting, N. B., Givvin, K. B., Sotelo, F. L., & Stigler, J. W. (2009). Teachers' Analyses of Classroom Video Predict Student Learning of Mathematics: Further Explorations of a Novel Measure of Teacher Knowledge. *Journal of Teacher Education, 61*(1-2), 172-181. doi:10.1177/0022487109347875

Knight, J. (2007). *Instructional coaching: A partnership approach to improving instruction.* Thousand Oaks, CA: Corwin.

Knight, J. (2009). Instructional coaching. In J. Knight (Ed.), *Coaching: Approaches and Perspectives* (pp. 29-55). Thousand Oaks, CA: Corwin.

Knight, J. (2011). *Unmistakable impact: a partnership approach for dramatically improving instruction.* Thousand Oaks, CA: Corwin.

Knight, J. (2014). *Focus on teaching: using video for high-impact instruction.* Thousand Oaks, CA: Corwin.

Knight, J. (2015). *Better conversations: coaching ourselves and each other to be more credible, caring, and contented.* Thousand Oaks, CA: Corwin.

Knight, J. (2017). *The Reflection Guide to the Impact Cycle What Instructional Coaches Should Do to Foster Powerful Improvements in Teaching.* Thousand Oaks, CA: Corwin.

Lesson Study Group at Mills College. (2015, October). Retrieved from http://lessonresearch.net/

Lewis, C. C. (2002). *Lesson study: A handbook of teacher-led instructional change.* Research for Better Schools.

Lewis, C. C., Perry, R., & Hurd, J. (2004). A deeper look at lesson study. *Educational leadership, 61*(5), 18.

Lewis, C. C., & Tsuchida, I. (1999). A Lesson Is Like a Swiftly Flowing River: How Research Lessons Improve Japanese Education. *Improving Schools, 2*(1), 48-56. doi:10.1177/136548029900200117

Little, J. W. (2002). Locating learning in teachers' communities of practice: opening up problems of analysis in records of everyday work. *Teaching and Teacher Education, 18*(8), 917-946. doi:10.1016/s0742-051x(02)00052-5

Santagata, R., & Guarino, J. (2011). Using video to teach future teachers to learn from teaching. *ZDM Mathematics Education, 43*(1), 133-145. doi:10.1007/s11858-010-0292-3

Santagata, R., & Yeh, C. (2014). Learning to teach mathematics and to analyze teaching effectiveness: Evidence from a video- and practice-based approach. *Journal of Mathematics Teacher Education, 17*(6), 491-514. doi:10.1007/s10857-013-9263-2

Santagata, R., Zannoni, C., & Stigler, J. W. (2007). The role of lesson analysis in pre-service teacher education: An empirical investigation of teacher learning from a virtual video-based field experience. *Journal of mathematics teacher education, 10*(2), 123-140.

Schön, D. A. (1983). *The reflective practitioner: how professionals think in action*. New York: Basic Books.

Seidel, T., Stürmer, K., Blomberg, G., Kobarg, M., & Schwindt, K. (2011). Teacher learning from analysis of videotaped classroom situations: Does it make a difference whether teachers observe their own teaching or that of others?. *Teaching and teacher education, 27*(2), 259-267.

Sherin, M. G. (2007). The development of teachers' professional vision in video clubs. *Video research in the learning sciences*, 383-395.

Sherin, M. G., & Han, S. Y. (2004). Teacher learning in the context of a video club. *Teaching and Teacher education, 20*(2), 163-183.

Sherin, M. G., & van Es, E. A. (2008). Effects of Video Club Participation on Teachers Professional Vision. *Journal of Teacher Education, 60*(1), 20-37. doi:10.1177/0022487108328155

Stepanek, J., Appel, G., Leong, M., Mangan, M. T., & Mitchell, M. (2006). *Leading lesson study: A practical guide for teachers and facilitators*. Corwin.

Stone, D., & Heen, S. (2015). *Thanks for the feedback: the science and art of receiving feedback well*. New York: Penguin.

Takahashi, A., & Mcdougal, T. (2016). Collaborative lesson research: maximizing the impact of lesson study. *ZDM Mathematics Education, 48*(4), 513-526. doi:10.1007/s11858-015-0752-x

Tripp, T. R., & Rich, P. J. (2012). The influence of video analysis on the process of teacher change. *Teaching and Teacher Education, 28*(5), 728-739. doi:10.1016/j.tate.2012.01.011

Using the classroom walk-through as an instructional leadership strategy. (2007, February). *The Center for Comprehensive School Reform and Improvement.*

van Es, E. A., & Sherin, M. G. (2002). Learning to notice: Scaffolding new teachers' interpretations of classroom interactions. *Journal of Technology and Teacher Education, 10*(4), 571-596.

van Es, E. A., & Sherin, M. G. (2008). Mathematics teachers' "learning to notice" in the context of a video club. *Teaching and Teacher Education, 24*(2), 244-276. doi:10.1016/j.tate.2006.11.005

van Es, E. A., & Sherin, M. G. (2010). The influence of video clubs on teachers' thinking and practice. *Journal of Mathematics Teacher Education, 13*(2), 155-176.

van Es, E. A., Tunney, J., Goldsmith, L. T., & Seago, N. (2014). A Framework for the Facilitation of Teachers' Analysis of Video. *Journal of Teacher Education, 65*(4), 340-356. doi:10.1177/0022487114534266

Waite, W. (2007). Using the classroom walk-through as an instructional leadership strategy. *The Center for Comprehensive School Reform.* Retrieved from https://eric.ed.gov/?id=ED495741

WestEd, Center for the Future of Teaching & Learning. (2016). Putting a lens on teacher practice: Video-based peer coaching. San Francisco, CA: WestEd.

ACKNOWLEDGMENTS

This book represents the combined knowledge from many years of interactions with educators and education scholars across the country. I am fortunate to have the opportunity to collaborate with many individuals, united by the shared vision of improving education options for all children.

First, I would like to thank Annie Lewis O'Donnell, my writing partner in the process of developing this book. With her help, we reached the finish line on time and with a manuscript stronger than I could have created on my own. I'm also grateful to Jim Knight for his ongoing collaboration about video coaching and his contribution to this book via the afterword. My thanks also go out to Debbie Armendariz, Suzanne Arnold, David Baker, Stacy Cope, Evelyn Cruz, Susanna Farmer, Amanda Huza, Nancy Jaeger, Megan Kelly-Petersen, Diane Lauer, Crystal McMachen, Kaleigh O'Donnell, Gayle Parenica, Robert Powell, Meghan Shaughnessy, and Rebekah Stathakis, who each contributed directly to this book through offering a story, a perspective, or even specific ideas for how to strengthen the manuscript.

The book creation process has been a team effort. Thanks to Kate Gagnon for encouraging me to undertake this project; to Nic Albert, our developmental editor, who ensured we clarified and strengthened our message; to Alan Hebel and Ian Koviak at The Book Designers for a strong cover design; and to Michele DeFilippo and Ronda Rawlins at 1106 Design who ensured that, literally, every single word appeared on the page.

I also want to thank Deborah Ball, Tim Boerst, Christina Brodbeck, Ron Fortune, Elham Kazemi, Daniel Kearns, Wendy Kopp, Eliot

147

Levinson, Shane Martin, Morva McDonald, Meri Tenney Muirhead, Gailene Nelson, Ted Quinn, Tom Stritikus, Kara Suzuka, and Jeff Wetzler, who have each influenced Edthena, often by changing my thinking about teacher professional development or challenging my ideas on how to create and run a company within the education sector.

Having so many individuals who are excited about video coaching and eager to support our endeavor is directly linked to the hard work of my team members. Becky Beauman, Erik Brown, Tanya Charkova, Rob Coplin, Kati Elliot, Kim Lanzilli, Christine Lynch, Anna Malsberger, Dan Moore, George Murray, Theresa Neil, Tarang Patel, Zac Stein, Ben Tomassetti, and Bill Townsley all helped build Edthena into what it is today. In addition, Dave Weldon, my co-founder, has been an invaluable partner and contributor to our success.

I'm thankful to the many teachers I have had throughout my education experience, including Susan Buchanan, Eileen Frey, Tom Fisher, Peter Filene, Ann Katabian, Glenn LaFerriere, and Mo Zoll, who each showed me what great teaching could look like and the impact great teaching can have on a student's trajectory.

Finally, thanks to my family and friends, my own coaches, who have encouraged me throughout the process of writing this book and along the way as we've built Edthena.

Made in the USA
Columbia, SC
06 November 2018